ENTHEOLOGUES

Conversations with Leading Psychedelic Thinkers, Explorers and Researchers

Featuring interviews with Rick Strassman, M.D., John Rush, Ph.D., Daniel Siebert, James Oroc and Jan Irvin

Edited by

Martin W. Ball, Ph.D.

Entheologues: Conversations with Leading Psychedelic Thinkers, Explorers and Researchers

Edited by
Martin W. Ball, Ph.D.

©2009 Martin Ball

Kyandara Publishing
ISBN: 978-0-578-03076-0

Cover art and design by Martin W. Ball

www.martinball.net
www.entheogenic.podomatic.com

Acknowledgments:

Thanks to James Oroc, Rick Strassman, Daniel Siebert, Jan Irvin and John Rush for allowing me to publish these interviews and your assistance in editing them. Thanks also to Realitysandwich.com for publishing the Strassman interview and my essay on entheogens and human rights. And thanks also to Timothy White for publishing the interview with Daniel Siebert in *Shaman's Drum* magazine. And of course, a special thanks to the listeners of the Entheogenic Evolution podcast for your interest and support in inspiring me to conduct these interviews in the first place.

Disclaimer:

TABLE OF CONTENTS

INTRODUCTION
- i

5-MEO-DMT – THE GOD MOLECULE
with James Oroc
- 1

VOYAGING TO DMT SPACE
with Dr. Rick Strassman, M.D.
- 34

GORDON WASSON, JOHN ALLEGRO AND THE HOLY
MUSHROOM
with Jan Irvin
- 65

MYCELIUM MESSIAH AND THE JESUS EXPERIENCE
with John R. Rush, Ph.D. N.D.
- 85

SALVIA DIVINORUM FROM A-Z
with Daniel Siebert
- 120

ENTHEOGENIC SPIRITUALITY AS A HUMAN RIGHT
by Martin W. Ball
- 151

INTRODUCTION

In January of 2008 I started The Entheogenic Evolution podcast with the intention of providing diverse information on the ritual and spiritual use of entheogens, along with the latest scientific research about these fascinating plants and chemicals. Over the past year, I've had the opportunity to interview a number of leading figures in the field of entheogen use and research as guests on the podcast. It is from this collection of interviews that I have gathered the materials for this book.

The idea to put together a book of transcripts of these interviews came when a technical flaw made my audio recordings of my interview with Dr. Rick Strassman unusable for the podcast. Despite my attempts at technical problem solving, the interview was plagued by strange pops and bleeps. It was far from listenable. Still wanting to share the interview, for which I had made a trip out to New Mexico to meet with Dr. Strassman in his home, I made a transcript of the interview and then read that on the podcast.

Not wanting all that effort of transcribing the interview to serve only the podcast (for anyone who hasn't been so lucky, the act of transcribing audio recordings is a long and tedious process), I decided to submit it to Realitysandwich.com for publication and was happy when it became one of their top stories of 2008. It was the widespread interest in having the written interview available that inspired me to take some of the other interviews from the podcast and transcribe them and present them as a book. You hold the results in your hands.

The interviews have undergone some editing to make ideas more complete and render the text more generally readable and have been reviewed by those interviewed. The conversational tone has been left intact and in some instances small additions have been made. The interview with Daniel Siebert has undergone the greatest amount of editing due to its publication in *Shaman's Drum*.

I have here dubbed these conversations "entheologues," being a combination of the term *entheogen*, meaning "generating the experience of the divine within" (and referring to psychedelic plants and mushrooms used in a spiritual fashion), and *dialogue*: thus these are conversations about the experience of the divine within. Each interviewee brings a different perspective and wealth of information about this fascinating topic.

The first entheologue features James Oroc, author of the new book *Tryptamine Palace*. Our conversation centers on the mystical experience occasioned by the ingestion of 5-MeO-DMT. Oroc claims that 5-MeO-DMT is the only true entheogen in that it can bring one into direct contact with God consciousness. To back up his claim, he dives into quantum physics and zero-point energy. Though "God" is not a term that is used often in entheogenic circles, despite the use of the term "entheogen," Oroc and I jump right into the broader questions of entheology and the nature of God in this unique conversation.

The second entheologue features Dr. Rick Strassman, M.D. For this interview, I traveled out to Dr. Strassman's home in New Mexico where we could sit and talk in the comfort of his living room. It was a true pleasure for me to meet Dr. Strassman in person, having emailed each other back and forth on occasion when I had questions for him about his research and work with DMT. Knowing of my own experience of working with 5-MeO-DMT (not the famed N,N-DMT of Dr. Strassman's research), one of Dr. Strassman's first questions for me after I arrived was whether I had ever seen "any of the little people" in my experiences. Though I hadn't, he had plenty to share from his own research into alien encounters and otherworldly journeys with DMT, the subject of his new edited book, *Inner Paths to Outer Space*.

In this interview, Dr. Strassman also discusses the trials and tribulations of trying to conduct entheogenic research in the U.S. and also raises the idea of entheogenic centers of learning. His current project is to create the Cottonwood Research Foundation for the study of psychedelics and entheogens where the subject could be approached from a more spiritual and therapeutic perspective than the model of research he was forced to follow in his DMT study.

The entheologue that follows features Jan Irvin from Gnosticmedia.com, who is deeply involved in researching the entheogenic origins of the Judeo-Christian tradition. For this interview, Irvin details the schism between one of the grandfathers of ethnomycology, Gordon Wasson, and the much-maligned John Marco Allegro, one of the original Dead Sea Scrolls scholars. Irvin has catalogued evidence that Wasson unfairly and somewhat unprofessionally bad-mouthed Allegro in the press for his claim that Jesus was not an historical person, but rather was, among other things, a symbolic representation of psychedelic mushrooms. In this fascinating interview, Irvin provides materials from his new book, *The Holy Mushroom*, where he successfully shows Wasson's critiques of Allegro to be unfounded and misinformed.

Continuing on the theme of the work of John Allegro, the fourth entheologue features professor John Rush, Ph.D., who discusses the ideas in his new book, *Failed God*. Rush goes a step beyond Allegro and argues that psychedelic sacraments form the basis of Judaism, Christianity, and Islam. He furthermore supports the position that neither Jesus nor Mohammed were historical figures and are mythological and symbolic creations associated with psychedelic plants and fungi. Intentionally provocative, Rush demands that scholars provide an explanation for the prevalence of psychedelic mushroom imagery in Christian art. To help illustrate his point, Dr. Rush has generously provided several original photographs that are included in his interview.

The fifth entheologue features Daniel Siebert from Sagewisdom.org, arguably the West's foremost expert on the entheogenic Mexican sage, *Salvia divinorum*. Siebert and I had first met in person in Southern California and had talked at length, so when I called him for this interview, I knew that could give a very complete picture of the history and uses of *Salvia divinorum* and Siebert did not disappoint. In his interview we learn everything from the indigenous context of *Salvia divinorum* to the history of how it was introduced to the West and it's possible medical uses. Siebert's thoroughness earned his interview the title of "*Salvia Divinorum* from A-Z." As this interview is also featured in the 2009 issue #79 of *Shaman's Drum* magazine, it's been edited a bit more than the other interviews.

The final chapter is an excerpt from my most recent book, *The Entheogenic Evolution: Psychedelics, Consciousness and Awakening the Human Spirit*. Though not an "entheoglogue" proper, I am including it here as much of what I write in the essay was inspired by the podcast and by the interviews presented in this book. I hope that the reader will find it a fitting conclusion to the wide variety of ideas and experiences presented in the entheologues. The essay is entitled "Entheogenic Spirituality as a Human Right" and is an edited section of the chapter "Shamans, Mystics and the Law" in *The Entheogenic Evolution*. The intent of the essay is to provide an overview of the cultural and historical background of the spiritual use of entheogens and then make a case for protecting entheogenic spirituality as a human right.

In many respects, this is my main goal: to have entheogenic spiritually recognized as a human right and have it protected by law. Though there have been recent gains in U.S. law with regard to entheogen use in the Native American Church and the Uniao Do Vegetal and Santo Daime churches, the recognition of the right to sacramental ingestion of entheogens is extremely limited. I strongly feel that the evidence is clear: humans have productively used entheogens for spiritual purposes for millennia and it is a foundational practice in the history of human spirituality and religion. The spiritual experiences generated by entheogens deserve to be recognized and protected by law and are fundamental to our religious freedom. The essay concludes with the "Universal Declaration of the Human Right to Direct Spiritual Experience."

I have also added on a new section to this essay that reviews the Santo Daime religious freedom case that was recently decided here in Medford and Ashland, Oregon, regarding members' of the Church of the Holy Light of the Queen right to the daime (ayahuasca) drink. It's a great pleasure to include this material given its timely relevance and my own personal connection to this church where I have had the extreme honor of drinking daime with a wonderful collection of truly good people.

It is my hope that this will be "volume one" of an ongoing series of books generated by interviews form The Entheogenic Evolution podcast. Interviews that have already been posted on the podcast but are not featured in this volume include Roland Griffiths and William Richards from Johns Hopkins University, author Thomas B. Roberts, Dr. Richard Grossman, and others. I invite readers to stop by the podcast for a listen, and feel free to suggest future guests and interviews to keep these dynamic entheologues going as we move forward to a day when entheogenic spirituality can be practiced openly and legally.

Enjoy the entheologues, and many blessings for your journey.

Martin W. Ball, editor

www.entheogenic.podomatic.com
www.martinball.net

5-MEO-DMT, THE GOD MOLECULE

An entheologue with

James Oroc

James Oroc is the author of the book, *Tryptamine Palace: 5-MeO-DMT and the Sonoran Desert Toad.* I've chosen the name for this interview in obvious reference to Rick Strassman's book, *DMT: The Spirit Molecule.* In that work, Strassman argued that N,N-DMT was the physical mechanism through which "spirit" might enter and exit the body. 5-MeO-DMT is far more powerful than N,N-DMT and often provides deep mystical experiences for users, many of whom claim, like Oroc, that it allows them to directly experience God. For this reason, I feel that it deserves the title I've given it here: the God molecule.

Martin Ball – My guest today is James Oroc. He's the author of the new book Tryptamine Palace, *which has just been released by Inner Traditions. Welcome to the Entheogenic Evolution podcast. It's a great pleasure to have you here.*

James Oroc – It's a pleasure to be here.

MB – To get us started, please tell us a little bit about yourself and your book, Tryptamine Palace, *which is largely about 5-MeO-DMT. Many people in the entheogenic community are familiar with N,N-DMT, usually just called "DMT," but not many people know much about 5-MeO-DMT, which is quite a different experience. How did you get into this relatively obscure, and tremendously powerful, entheogen?*

JO – I decided to write a book about it because the first time I tried 5-MeO-DMT, I had the most significant spiritual and entheogenic experience of my life. It was much different than any other experience I'd ever had on any other entheogen. It pretty much caused my worldview to collapse, at that time, and then I needed to discover a new worldview that made sense of my experiences.

So my book, *Tryptamine Palace*, is the result of 5 years of research and thought and experimentation into rebuilding my worldview in a way so that I could actually live with my experiences; something I think I've successfully done using a lot of the cutting edge discoveries of science, especially quantum physics, and with an increased interest in the history of mysticism, which I think has a lot to do with the kinds of experiences I've been having, and others have been having, on 5-MeO-DMT.

My original inspiration to write the book – I am actually an author and extreme sports journalist and I've been writing and traveling for most of the past 25 years – but my inspiration was Burning Man. I'm a very keen participant in the Burning Man movement and I wanted to write a book for Burning Man. As an artist, I figured that that hadn't actually been done, giving out a book as a playa gift. So I wrote the first edition of *Tryptamine Palace* and gave away 250 copies the first year on the playa. Then I worked on it more and gave away 250 more copies of the second edition.

Eventually it fell into the hands of John Hannah, a very fine editor, and he worked on it with me for quite a while. We were about to go into the self-publishing process, which I was very excited about, but I figured I'd better toughen up as an author and I'd send it off to a couple of publishers just to get used to getting rejected. To my surprise, Inner Traditions accepted the book, which was a huge shock to my system – as you can imagine. Since that time there have been six more edits, with two of Inner Tradition's editors. So in total, the book has had nine edits with three editors to reach its current state, so it has evolved a long way from the original one that circulated on the playa that you're familiar with.

MB – Yes, I've seen several different versions now and I would have to say, I've really enjoyed seeing the editing process and what's been done with the book. I've enjoyed the book from the beginning, but I would have to say that it's a stronger book now. They've done an excellent job of working with you, despite the fact that it's taken a long time – I know that must be somewhat frustrating. But it's a very good book.

JO – Thank you. It's been hard work. I wouldn't say it's been frustrating because it's been a steady flow of information coming in. The way the information has channeled itself into writing this book has been very unusual for me as a writer. I actually feel like the book is a fairly good summary of where my own views on the subject are at and it's a lot fuller than the original versions. So I'm very happy about that. Plus, I got to work with some really amazing editors - Inner Traditions actually gave me Nancy Yeilding to work with, who is Ervin Lazlo's editor. It was Laszlo's books on the Akashic Field that made me send *Tryptamine Palace* to Inner Traditions in the first place, I think he is undoubtedly one of the greatest thinkers on the planet these days and one of the few heroes I have, so it was a great honor to work with one of his editors. Inner Traditions was just great to work with.   They were very supportive and they have a lot of great authors on their imprint, so I was very honored to be included in that category. It made me work a lot harder.

MB – That definitely is a great honor. I'd like to hear more about some of the ideas in the book, but let's step back in time, before we get there, because you've already mentioned here about how your first experience with 5-MeO-DMT was substantially different from any of your other experiences with entheogens. This is definitely an impression that I would have to second for myself. My first experience with 5-MeO was quite radical and my impression was that this was complete mystical absorption and it extended far beyond any other medicine I had ever used. But for yourself, what were some of the experiences that you had prior to working with 5-MeO-DMT? What kinds of medicines had you worked with and how would you compare the 5-MeO experience?

JO – Well, when I was in my twenties, I was very enthusiastic about entheogens of all shapes and sizes. I was a big fan of Terence McKenna. I had spent some time in South America. I was very interested in continuing investigations in shamanism and had some discussions with Mark Plotkin at some point and was actually trying to move to Ecuador in 1996 to continue this work when a series of personal disasters didn't allow that. I turned my back on South America, and kind of turned my back on entheogens for quite a while, or they faded in their significance for me as I had other things going on in my life that seemed more important. And I have to say that at the point where I tried the 5-MeO-DMT, I was several years passed any point where I thought that entheogens really had a lot more for me. I thought I had learned a lot of what they had to teach me and I was more interested in things like yoga and meditation – I guess more traditional methods of exploring the psyche.

I had looked for DMT for a number of years, like many of us, and it was an extremely hard drug to find. Of course, it's not legal, which doesn't help, but in other countries and other places I looked for it pretty thoroughly, with no success, to the point that I actually gave up. And then several years later I was dating a girl (who is now actually my wife), and she got a phone call from one of her best friends, who had just smoked 5-MeO-DMT, and it was obviously a life-changing experience for him. One of the things that happens when you first smoke 5-MeO, and I've heard this from quite a few different people, is you see the faces of some of your closest and dearest friends and family and when you come out of it, you feel, "Oh my God, I've got to tell these people about what just happened to me!" So this character called up my to-be wife in the middle of the night and was ranting and raving about the breadth of his experience. When I saw her the next day she told me that her friend had just smoked this DMT stuff and it sounded amazing. My reaction was, "DMT! I've been looking for that for years!"

MB – At that point, had you heard of the radical difference between 5-MeO-DMT and N,N-DMT?

JO – I knew nothing. I didn't even know 5-MeO existed. So I got in touch with this friend and he told me that this DMT, 5-MeO-DMT, was legally available on the internet, which it was for a short window between 1995 and 2002 or 2003, as far as I can tell. So I immediately ordered some up, and when I was waiting for it to arrive, I started doing some research and realized that this was actually a lot different from what I thought it was. So I didn't immediately do it.

The more potent cousin of N,N-DMT is the lesser-known 5-MeO-DMT. If N,N is the "spirit molecule," 5-MeO could be the "God molecule."

The small amount of 5-MeO in this vial is sufficient for 2-3 doses.

Sometime later I went out to Oregon to visit with a friend and he gave me the instructions on how to do it. I ended up doing it with another friend, and none of us had done it before. Our instructions were pretty loose. My impression from reading Terence McKenna's stuff was that it was going to be a cross between a bong hit and doing a hit of acid (LSD). We weighed out a tenth of a gram and eyed it out into 4 piles since we didn't have the proper scales, and since I was going first and wanted to make sure that I got off, I took the biggest pile – a classic beginner's mistake.

About 40 minutes later I came to in the corner of my friend's little office in Portland, with he and his brother cowering in amazement in the corner. I'd pretty much trashed most of the room. I'd been doing Maori war dances and sun salutations and screaming to the heavens. And I must say it was the most surprised I've ever been in my life from any singular experience. And from that every first experience, I believed I had come in contact with the Godhead, or God consciousness, or just plain God, if you want. Since I was a pretty hard core atheist, at that point in time, having been brought up in the scientific/rationalist mindset, this was an enormous surprise for me because I didn't believe in God, yet here I was having experienced it. So that was the first thing that caused my worldview to start crumbling down, and everything since then has been a search for answers and explanations for where this substance takes me and how I think I can resonate with this God energy.

Now, one of the things I've come to realize is that talking about God is probably the most difficult thing you can talk about in this day and age. It's really one word that has enormous power. You just mention the word "God" amongst people and they stiffen and I know because I was the same way. Before I smoked 5-MeO-DMT, if you had told me that you had experienced the Godhead, I would have laughed at you and said, "Well, that's your illusion." And I find that when I speak about this substance, about 95% of the room looks at me like I'm mad and there's usually one person who comes up and says, "Yeah, I know exactly what you're talking about. I've been to that place."

And you, Martin, are actually my favorite example because when you guys first discussed *Tryptamine Palace* on this podcast, I could tell you were interested in my ideas but I could also hear that there was a certain amount of resistance.

MB – Because I had not been there, yet.

JO – No. You had a large number of your own experiences – a lifetime – to write against my experience. No one ever wants to think that nothing we've ever done is like this other thing. If you read Stanislav Grof, certainly other people have experienced this sort of thing on other entheogens, but for me, 5-MeO-DMT is the most effective. And when you experienced it for yourself a couple of months after discussing the book, I got your email the next day and you were like, "Wow – now I know exactly what you're talking about!" and I had to laugh because I knew that you had gone to the exact same place that I have and you were just as mystified about it as I was.

MB – And as I wrote you in my email, the first thing that came out of my mouth was just "Thank you, God!" That was the word that came out. And I had struggled with that word for my entire life, exactly as you're describing. It made me very uncomfortable. I didn't like it when people talked about God. I grew up an atheist and when I got into spirituality as an adult, I was much more comfortable with terms like "universal consciousness" or "Buddha mind" or something like that. But when I had 5-MeO-DMT and the full experience, "God" is the word that I had to say because it was true. This is God and there's absolutely no question about it. So that definitely changed me, pretty much immediately.

JO – One of the things that I've been fascinated about most recently is the relationship between language and tryptamines. There are a lot of people, Mark Pesce and other writers, who are definitely drawing these links that somewhere in the tryptamine experience the human mind managed to link meanings with symbols and noise and I honestly believe that "God" was the first word.

Whatever entheogenic experience kicked off this radical experiment in human consciousness, I believe the first word uttered by the shaman would have been "God," because what else are you going to say? If you've touched this experience and your cerebral cortex is now stimulated in a way it's never been stimulated, I honestly believe that this was the first word and everything's come from there. And it's the word that comes out in these experiences.

I actually stand up in my 5-MeO experiences and say the world "God," apparently. One of the things about a 5-MeO experience is you need to rely on your friends to tell you what you did as you may not remember.

But I find the whole relationship with the word fascinating and that is still caries such power. You know, I wrote an article for *The Entheogen Review*, "Where is God in the Entheogenic Movement?" because I find it interesting that we use the word "entheogen," which means "god generated within" or "god carried within," yet we're very uncomfortable talking about God, even within the entheogenic movement.   I went to the World Psychedelic Conference in Basil, and you didn't hear the word mentioned hardly at all.   Everybody wants to talk about everything else; cluster headaches, tryptamine elves, transmissions from the Pleiades, and every other bloody thing you can think of.   But the thing were all really interested in, I think, is the source of spirituality and the source of all this, and my 5-MeO experiences definitely make me believe in a field of energy that I know as God.   And I think that historically, all religions, all mystics, all shamans, have tapped into this same field of energy and they all come back calling it the same thing and we just get mixed up from that point on. As Colin Wilson wrote "Religion starts as a clear mountain river, and becomes a slow muddy stream."

MB – This is one of the reasons why I'd really like to see more people have the opportunity to experience 5-MeO-DMT. I think that it could really help cut out the middle man of concepts that we have here when people do want to talk about the Pleiades and the machine elves and the Gaian spirits, or whatever. The source of all of it is what we can certainly identify as God. You can have the experience, recognize it for what it is, and identify it. Let's open up our language and not be so shy about using the word. So I definitely applaud you for that. It's one of the things that I really love most about your book. You're not shy about it and you set it right up front and say, "Look – this is a true entheogen and that means it takes you to an experience of God, and this is what it is."

JO – I think, for me, 5-MeO-DMT was the only substance interesting and powerful enough that it made me write a book.   With my experiences on all the other things, I didn't feel that I was going to add to the body of work that is already out there. But the opportunity was presented for this book and I think it was that central experience, what I honestly believe is the ultimate experience of being human now. If you can experience the Godhead in your life, your life is radically changed.

MB – Right, because that's who and what you really are. That's your true core. It's about experiencing ourselves in our true nature.

JO – And experiencing that brings such peace of mind and such energy and a sense of responsibility, as well. And all those things are classic spiritual epiphanies, so it certainly fits into a class mystical experience. It fulfills the phenomenological framework of those experiences that we know about from history.

This is why I've been so fascinated with the mystical experience. I'm actually much more interested in mysticism than I am in, let's say, shamanism. I think "shaman" is probably one of the most abused terms in the English language, at the moment, especially on the west coast. It's unfortunate, but I think that we relate to shamanism because it's a technology. With our mindset in the 21st century, we're used to technologies, and the thought that plants are technology and the thought that the shaman is a kind of technician really appeals to a lot of us. But mystics aren't technicians. Mystics are working in a zone that is very hard to explain, very hard to translate, and it's a totally different thing.

I think in the west we actually come much more from the mystical tradition, all the way back to Lucius and the Greeks, and our own society has not had a lot of shamans and shamanistic traits for a long, long time. But mysticism is something that's been buried in our society, even in Christianity, all the way to the current time.

Because of the book, some people like to say that I'm a shaman. I'm definitely not a shaman. I've zero ability to heal that I know of and I don't have a lot of personal interest in shamanism. I prefer to consider myself a modern mystic, at this point.

MB – I think that something else that's a little bit more appealing about shamanism to people in New Age circles is that they can get into spirituality while avoiding this word "God" and the reality of God and they can talk about spirits and visions and all the rest of this stuff, but not really get to the core, which is the Divine Being. They can just avoid all that language and it becomes much more comfortable for people.

JO – I would agree with that. I also find it interesting that I've done ayahuasca in South America, in Ecuador and Peru, and I've never had much luck with it. My system doesn't seem to work that well with that medicine. But having watched a number of indigenous ceremonies, I noticed that, (and not only with ayahuasca but also with peyote and San Pedro and other things), shamans traditionally don't take their patients to a psychedelic state. They use a very small amount of the entheogen. It's usually fairly homeopathic, and I think it's more about bringing the energy fields of the patient in line with the energy field of the shaman. The shaman has reached this state by doing gallons and gallons and gallons of ayahuasca over several years when they've been training, and they can almost induce that state at will. So they only need their patient to be in a fairly homeopathic state. They only need a little bit.

I believe this relates to the idea of consciousness being a Bose-Einstein condensate within the neurons of the brain – a highly 'coherent' field, where the neurons in the brain all act in unison. It has been proven that a higher, more ordered Bose-Einstein condensate – i.e. a more coherent consciousness – can cause less organized fields to become more organized – more coherent. I believe the shaman, or the Hindu saddhu, or meditation master in Tibet, all possess more coherent Bose-Einstein condensates within the neuron patterns in their brains, which they have achieved from their years of discipline and training.

When a student, or patient, becomes exposed to the Master's Bose-Einstein condensate, or consciousness-field if you prefer, then their own consciousness-field will naturally want to become more organized, more coherent, and more able to let the light of inner consciousness in. If you introduce a homeopathic amount of an entheogen that the Master/Shaman is trained in to his patient/student, then this tendency towards coherence, and ultimately resonance, is increased. You hear this expressed all the time when normal people come in the presence of high Masters ... people often come away saying they were speechless, some how overwhelmed merely being close to a more evolved consciousness ...and I believe that it is bringing the field of the shaman and the patient into coherence that is the basis of all shamanic healing, with or without entheogens,

Now when your Westerner goes to a shaman, they don't want to get healed, they want to get high. The Peruvian and Ecuadorian Shamans have all figured this out, and I believe that they're definitely cranking the brews way up because they know that Westerner's want to experience the psychedelic.

If you read Terence's original account in the Archaic Revival when he talks about going to Colombia in the 70's, his whole crew did ayahuasca down there and nobody got off. It was only went they brought several bottles of it back to the states and kept upping the dose that he finally got an effect similar to when he was smoking DMT. But if you read traditional accounts, such as Richard Evan Shultes, he never got high on ayahuasca. He named the *Banisteriopsis caapi*, but all he ever experienced was some colors and some squiggly lines, which is about all I've ever had. So I think that it's interesting that we have such an ayahuasca movement sweeping the country, but it isn't being used the way I think it was traditionally used.

The shaman in a healing circle is certainly not taking ayahuasca to the point where he's tripping. He's only taking it to the point where he can still interact. He's definitely still in control of his own experience.

MB – From a larger sociological perspective, something that I feel is that Westerners need strong trips and they need to purge, actually. In that sense, ayahuasca can be very useful for people because in Western society, we have a lot of garbage that we need to clean out and we have a lot of mental blocks to overcome in opening to spiritual experience. Perhaps we need stronger doses because we're further removed from the reality that it opens us up to than indigenous people in the local village.

JO – It knocks us out of our rationalist box. Jeremy Narby's tale in *The Cosmic Serpent* is probably the best account of this. Here's a guy who's a Swiss/Canadian scientist, totally rigid. He's living with the tribes for three years and he keeps asking them how they learn all about the plants, and the shamans tell him that it's the ayahuasca that tells them. His reaction is like, "Yeah, right. How do you really learn?" This claim doesn't make sense in his worldview so he dismisses it.

On the last day, the shaman obviously cooks him up a good brew, which knocks him completely out of his box, and he has an experience very similar to mine where he spends the next few years trying to put his worldview back together in a way that makes sense to him. In doing so, he comes up with some fascinating ideas about the relationship between DNA and tryptamines, which I used as a lead to follow up further in my own investigations. Narby's ideas about the bio-photonic emission of DNA – the idea that DNA actually emits light – led me to my own investigation into the zero-point field.

MB – Well let's come back to some of these more scientific ideas but maybe first we can talk about what the 5-MeO-DMT experience is like for you.

JO – The experience is very overwhelming and it goes through a series of phases. Once you breathe out the 5-MeO, you tend to enter a tunnel of light. There'll be an experience of being surrounded by multitudes – all your friends and all the people who love you. For me, they're usually telling me that I've "gotten it right" or that I've "understood the answer" or I've "figured it out," and now all I need to do is relax and let go.

When you can do that, you dissolve into the next level, where things get really strange. But the height of the experience for me is the experience of being pure consciousness, with no memory of who I am or where I came from, with no ego attached. It's simply "I am . . ." and I'm conscious of everything at once. It feels like you have the breadth of the entire universe contained within your consciousness, and it's an extraordinarily overwhelming experience. At the height of that, I start to freak out. I think, "How did this start? Where did I come from? Who am I? I've got this much knowledge! What in the hell is going on here?" And that's usually when a little voice comes in and says, "Remember – you smoked the DMT." About 5 seconds later I'm on the floor in a crumpled heap, completely dropped out of the zone.

I've found very interesting similarities between this experience and Hinduism and Buddhism and various other mystical traditions. Having experienced this, I then needed some answers. How did I get access to this unlimited zone of information? How could I exist as consciousness without ego? How could I really associate this with God? Because that's what the end realization is: this state of pure consciousness that you are in is actually the God state and you are resonating with everything, which is God, and God is actually you. You're just a little sensory organ attached to this infinite zone.

So I went looking for answers to explain this. We've been brought up in the Western, Newtonian, rational viewpoint that everything is force and reaction and all that really exists in the universe is physical qualities and all these non-physical qualities we just ignore. That wasn't really going to work for the experience that I had. So I went looking for answers that made more sense.

The first person I got turned onto was David Bohm, an amazing physicist, who came out with a book, *Wholeness and the Implicate Order*. His idea was that in the universe there had to be a series of dimensions surrounding us that create the order and information that streams into our universe to keep it intact. And that Wholeness is actually a great deal more than the physical dimensions we occupy. Some thirty years ago Bohm predicted that a vast underlying field of energy must exist. And now in the last fifteen years, the existence of this field has been proven.

This is a realization that's has only occurred in the last decade or so. We've increasingly come to realize that there is a field of energy called the "zero-point field," or "scalar field" or "Akashic field" – it has a number of different names – but this is now a scientifically proven field of energy. It isn't a theory. We know it exists. It's the underlying field of energy that exists prior to all the other energies of the universe, and that all energy and matter in our universe comes constantly in and out of in the form of virtual particles.

The best way of understanding this as a metaphor is if you took a cubic meter or square foot of space and you sucked every molecule out of that space and you made it a vacuum so that there was technically zero matter left in it, there is still a steady pulse of energy that comes out of this vacuum. This is what we call the zero-point energy field.

What's been going on for about 80 years is physicists have just been ignoring it. They've known that this exists, but physicists have felt that it messed up all their calculations, so they've just zeroed it out. All the energy coming in was equal to the energy going out, so let's just zero it out and ignore it.

In the last 20 years they've come realize that there is a lot more going on there than they thought. What we now believe is that all matter and energy and information in our universe comes in and out of this zero-point field as virtual electrons and virtual protons. So there's this unbelievably rapid exchange of energy and information that's constantly going on at the rate of a billionths of a second. But everything that we experience in this universe is originating out of this base field of energy. It's that field of energy that I believe that you end up resonating with in the 5-MeO-DMT experience.

Ervin Lazlo has written several books on this subject. He has expanded the concept and renamed it the akashic field, which is taken from the Hindu concept of *akasha*. Hindus believed that akasha was a subtle field of energy that permeated throughout the entire universe and it carried all that was to come and all that came before. Every experience went into the field and was recorded there in the akashic library as an imprint. Now, modern science is increasingly agreeing with this idea that the zero-point field or the akashic field as a field of energy that every experience that has happened gets recorded in. But this underlying field of energy not only has a record of everything that has happened in our universe in all time, but quite possibly contains everything that is going to happen in the future, as well. It's like a sea of potentiality or possibility out of which the universe arises as an instance of actuality.

The existence of this vast field of energy seemed to answer a few of my questions. And then I started to investigate the idea that consciousness is actually a quantum phenomenon. This is where Jeremy Narby's ideas of DNA and bio-photonic emission come in. But basically the idea is that our brain is actually an antenna. Consciousness isn't contained in the brain. Consciousness is contained within this zero-point field and our brain acts as an antenna that picks up this field. That happens through the neurons in our brains, which are more numerous than all the stars in the galaxy. They act as tiny antennas and they pick up information from the field and send it back in. Thus one potential view is that consciousness is not actually a phenomenon caused by the matter in our brain, but that our brain is simply a mechanism required to interpret consciousness.

MB – This is a point that I also like to emphasize. For all the sophisticated neuroscience that we have, there actually is no evidence that consciousness is produced by the brain. There's no reason to believe that unless you choose to believe it, but the scientific evidence is clearly lacking. The model of the brain as a receiver or filter of consciousness works equally as well as saying that it's produced by the brain, and in fact, it's probably better because there is no evidence that consciousness is produced by the brain. There is no mechanism for that. All we have are descriptions of neurons and how energy is working in the brain, but not the production of consciousness.

JO – There's that great quote out of Aldous Huxley's final book *Island* that I start '*Tryptamine Palace*' with, in which one of the main characters states "*You're assuming that the brain produces consciousness. I'm assuming it transmits consciousness. And my explanation is no more far-fetched than yours... You can't demonstrate the truth in your hypothesis, and I can't demonstrate the truth of mine. And even if you could prove me wrong, would it make any practical difference?* And while Huxley wrote that over 40 years ago, I don't think the situation has really changed amongst consciousness researchers.

For anyone who's interested in the concept of a quantum basis for consciousness, should read the book, *The Quantum Self*, by Dana Zohar. It's a great book and she comes up with a very feasible model of a quantum mechanism for consciousness. One of the things that she brings up is the concept of the Bose-Einstein condensate, which I mentioned before, which is when a quantum system made up of individuals acts as a singular coherent unit. For example, let's say that all the neurons in your brain are like little compasses individually spinning around, and imagine that you had a way to get all of them to set to north. All of the neurons in your brain effectively start working as one neuron, and that's called a Bose-Einstein condensate.

Now this traditionally has been thought only to exist in superconductors and things that work at absolute zero. What happens at this state is if you have billions of helium atoms, when they reach absolute zero, they form a Bose-Einstein condensate. They work as one helium atom in the sense that they are no longer individuals. So with Dana Zohar's concept is that the more coherent our neurons, the more stable of a Bose-Einstein condensate exists. The stronger this Bose-Einstein condensate is, the more interaction you're going to be able to have with the field.

I believe that when you smoke 5-MeO-DMT, this causes all the neurons in your brain to snap into a super Bose-Einstein condensate with complete resonance with the zero-point field. Now they believe the mechanism of the zero-point field is also a Bose-Einstein condensate that mirrors the Bose-Einstein condensate of our brain. So going back to the old Hermetic concept of "As above, so below," human consciousness is actually a microcosmic replica of the consciousness of the zero-point energy field of the whole universe, which is what I would call God consciousness, if I were looking for the word.

So the idea that 5-MeO-DMT can allow me to experience this field of God consciousness suddenly makes sense. The Bose-Einstein condensate of my mind is mirroring that Bose-Einstein condensate of the zero-point field. They've effectively become one and I've ceased to exist, other than as part of the greater consciousness. As I've said, your ego gets left behind. You don't exist. Consciousness exists, but you don't know who you are or where you came from. You are One with Oneness, there is no room for 'You' anymore. I believe that tryptamines, 5-MeO-DMT and N,N-DMT, are very effective ego-destroyers. What they really do is they wipe away the ego shell and reveal the inner consciousness.

Ekhart Tolle's book, *New Awakening,* has got a lot of good ideas on the ego shell and structure. He makes no mention of entheogens in the book, but I think his ideas are very relevant for anyone interested in experimenting with tryptamines. It's often more interesting to read books like that investigating the role of the ego than it is to read books investigating the role of drugs, per se.

MB – I would have to agree with you. I haven't read much of Tolle's work, but from what I have seen, I would have to agree that he does a really excellent job of dealing with the ego in relation to cosmic consciousness. This is a topic that should be discussed more in entheogenic circles, as it's more useful than just seeking after visionary experiences and big trips.

JO – Everyone out there dealing with tryptamines should read *New Awakenings.*

MB – They really should check out his work, and it's even better that he's not dealing with entheogens because then he's not really getting caught in ideas of astral realms and all the rest of this. He's just dealing with ego versus unitary consciousness: what's the difference, how do we get there, what does it mean for our lives? In that sense, he's providing a very practical entry into more mystical participation and mystical consciousness.

JO – I didn't read *The Power of Now* fully, but when I read *New Awakening*, his second book, the impression I got was that the first book was for people on the path, whereas *New Awakening* is for people who've actually arrived. The concepts he was working with there just rang like a bell in my head as so much of what he wrote was similar to the ideas I'd been working with and going through in my own mind. His whole thing is that we're at a point where human consciousness is flowering and we're entering into a new era for human consciousness. I certainly believe that tryptamines are doing their part to stimulate human consciousness at this very critical juncture in history.

MB – I think they're absolutely fundamental. There's something very, very special about the tryptamines. I think that it has to do with the fact that we already have the tryptamines in our bodies – we're designed for them. All mammals, humans included, naturally produce DMT. So there's a very special resonance.
There's an idea I wanted to share with you in dealing with the conception of consciousness as being filtered through the brain but actually coming from somewhere else. I think that something significant about tryptamines is that they're actually microscopic crystals. When we're ingesting N,N-DMT or 5-MeO-DMT, we're putting these crystalline substances into our body. From a very general perspective, we can say that crystals transmit, conduct, and focus energy. So really what we're doing is we're putting these little crystal receptors on our neurons in our brain and this is allowing us to resonate with this God field of energy. The tryptamines are changing the resonance fields of our physical bodies to allow us to access that conscious state at that quantum level.

JO – According to Jeremy Narby, you can even consider DNA to be a crystal.

MB – It certainly makes sense. What we're dealing with here is our interaction with an energetic source. The Divine Being, ultimately, is energy, as you're describing with the zero-point energy field. God is the source of all the energy that comprises the physical world as well as the energy of life and consciousness.

A questions then arises: how does this energy translate from this energetic source into an embodied, physical form? Well, you need crystalline structures to help transmit and focus that energy. So we can look at our DNA as crystals. Our bodies are mostly salt water, which is a combination of two crystals, water and salt. In a sense, we are liquid crystal physical forms and when we add a little bit more of these very important crystals such as DMT or 5-MeO, then we can radically change our consciousness and our resonant field and commune with in the cosmic mind. Really tryptamines are crystals that allow us to access the Divine Imagination in the visionary state and also open us to the direct apprehension of archetypal (or pre-form, implicate) God energy.

JO – One of the main proposals in my book – and I think this is probably the only original idea I have had – is that 5-MeO-DMT increases the coherence of the Bose-Einstein condensate in the neurons in the brain, which increases an individual consciousnesses resonance with the Bose-Einstein condensate of the zero-point field – which is the consciousnesses of the Universe, perhaps even a layer of the consciousness of God. That's what I believe happens when you smoke 5-MeO-DMT – your mind resonates with the mind of God, the mind of everything, it resonates with all available energy and information. I think it's Lynn McTaggert in the book *The Field*, which is one of the first really good books written about the zero-point field and is probably the best book to read to enter into this subject as it's written from a layman's perspective (she's a journalist), where she says that all energy and matter could simply be consciousness trying to deal with these streams of information. I find it interesting that we use the term crystallization as if the universe of matter has crystallized out of this energy field of possibility. And I think that this is really the crux – the zero-point field is the field of all potentiality and all possibility.

The universe, or God in its most infinite, most expansive state, would be a flat featureless field of everything. Now that's pretty dull. You actually need something to happen. So our universe is the universe of happening. We're the actuality. Potentiality be damned. We're the thought that rippled through the Field – the desire, the notion, whatever it is, that has managed to pull itself out of total potential to actually become something.

MB – *Which is the point.*

JO – Exactly. That's the most amazing thing. As the Dalai Lama say "This is existence – and it is a very special thing. A bridge between the finite and the infinite." We're in this constant going in and out of this field, because we're informing this field and we're allowing the field the ability to realize its full potential, which is God realizing its potential. That's basically how I envision our existence now.

MB – *A way that I like to think of it is that through our own evolution in physical reality, in a sense, God is also evolving in physical reality, because if God is the absolute state of all potential, nothing actually happens there. It's all just potential until something happens, which is us and the physical universe we live in. We're the ones that are actually happening, and through our knowledge and our experience, we are evolving the ultimate potential of the Divine to manifest in the physical world.*

JO – And we're sending in the report.

MB – *Yes. It's this back-and-forth between manifest actuality and infinite potentiality, and if we can do this in a conscious way, which is what things like 5-MeO help us to awaken to, then we can become more conscious participants in the process. But this also means that we have a hell of a lot of responsibility. We're responsible because we are God in embodied form, and this comes with free will. So we are responsible for our actions and our choices.*

JO – That's another very interesting thing to me. One of the most obvious things that has happened to me since my experiences with 5-MeO-DMT is an extremely increased sense of responsibility for myself, for my planet, for my people, for a lot of things. I found a parallel to this in something called Liberation Theology, which is this idea that if you have a true spiritual epiphany, then you don't have any choice but to get active. The amount of responsibility that is then put on you requires that you do something. And there's this idea of contemplative activists like the Dalai Lama, Martin Luther King Jr, Ghandi, Thomas Merton, Mother Theresa, Thich Nhat Hanh, not to mention the nameless Buddhist monks in Mynamar, or the Qui Gong masters in China – all of these people are contemplative activists. It's their relationship with God that gives them the responsibility and the ability to actually go and do all the unbelievable things that they do.

This is a very important fact about 5-MeO and tryptamines and ayahuasca and all these things. If you have a true spiritual epiphany, your life is changed. You're not just going to go back to work on Monday and have things be business as usual. It just doesn't work like that. You don't have the choice. It's not like, "Oh, maybe I'll do something about the state of the planet." You're really pushed in that direction, and I honestly think that that's a big part of what's going on.

I think it's very interesting that in the same era that we split the atom and some of the most terrifying things are going on, we've synthesized mescaline, discovered LSD, and realized the universality of DMT. So within that same forty years, it's like the yin and yang – we have the terrifying energy of nuclear weapons and then we have this intellectual energy that's entered our society on the opposite end that's ultimately the most awakening energy possible. Many people believe the entire ecology movement evolved out of the mass use of LSD in the 60's and 70's, that our whole sense of Gaia, of the earth as a single living organism, came out of the generational revelations of LSD, mescaline, and magic mushrooms.

I doubt that anybody who ever smoked 5-MeO-DMT could use a nuclear weapon. I think every world leader everywhere should A, drop some acid, and B, smoke some 5-MeO-DMT. Their ability to make war would be radically diminished. It's a spiritual and mental position that you reach, and there's no going back. I think that's actually one of the hardest things about 5-MeO-DMT: are you going to believe what happened to you? Are you truly going to believe that you've experienced God within yourself and your ultimate connection to everything that exists? Because if you believe, then everything has changed. If you just say, "Well, that was kinda fun, and it was interesting but it doesn't mean anything," then you can slide back into your old life. I don't see that happening very often.

MB – Right. That's so hard to do with 5-MeO. People need to understand that if you take this, you are committing to changing your consciousness and your life. This is a huge step.

JO – Quite possibly. It doesn't happen to everyone. I am a big fan of the ideas of the American psychologist Abraham Maslow, as are people like the existentialist writer Colin Wilson, and the visionary artists, Alex and Allyson Grey. Maslow saw human existence as a pyramid, where the smallest number of the population, the tip of the iceberg, manage to escape the biological fight for survival and reach the ultimate human state of transcendence, a state he called 'self-actualization'. Self-actualized people are assumed to be rare in Maslow's model – as little as 5% of the population. This 5% is thought to control the direction and destiny of the species. Now within this 5%, there is an even smaller group – 5% of 5% - that turn their backs on wealth and power – the usual rewards of being part of the dominant minority – in search of what Maslow calls the highest of human experiences – the "peak experience".

So you could say that all 5-MeO-DMT smokers are seeking a "peak" experience, and many of them will find that experience within 5-MeO-DMT. However, according to Maslow there are 2 types of "peak" experiences – the relative and the absolute. Relative experiences characterize those peak experiences in which there remains an awareness of subject and object, and which are thus extensions of the individual's own experience's. Maslow says "(They) are not a true mystical experiences, but inspirations, ecstasies, and raptures" and I believe this is what happens to the majority of 5-MeO smokers ... they have a peak experience, its relative, not absolute. However for a very small percent of 5-MeO-DMT users, the 5% of the 5%, there is a peak experience beyond the relative, the Absolute, which according to Maslow "are characteristic of mystical experiences, and are comparable to the experiences of the great mystics in history. They are timeless, spaceless, and characterized by unity, in which the subject and object become one."

For a very small percentage of 5-MeO users, this absolute mystical experience can happen, and there is nothing that you can do to be ready for that. If that happens, your life is changed. I know, because the last five years of my life have undeniably been affected by 5-MeO-DMT!

MB – As has mine. You know, I've seen plenty of people experience 5-MeO who haven't quite been prepared for the commitment it can bring. They start waking up in the middle of the night and find that they're tripping just as hard as they did on their journey and they really struggle with it. Perhaps they're trying to compartmentalize it and saying to themselves, "OK, that was just the 5-MeO and I don't have to deal with that in everyday reality," but if you open yourself up to that, you have to be prepared. It can really challenge you and transform how you understand who you are and how you look at pretty much everything.

JO – And that can be positive or it can be negative. There's a very interesting book called *Darkness Shining Wild* by Robert Augustus Masters. It's entirely about his negative experience with 5-MeO-DMT. What's interesting is that when I read his accounts, it's as though we've had identical experiences, but he found nothing but terror and I found nothing but joy. I cannot explain to you how that happened or why that happened. He's so terrified by the same things that I found liberating and they are very similar experiences. It spun him out for some time and got him on anti-psychotic medicines, and this was someone who was into yoga and meditation and such. I really don't have any explanation for that.

In the new version of the book, I have a series of appendices, and one of them is on that book and it's called "Heaven and Hell" and is a recognition of the fact that the experience can seriously challenge some people. I'm very wary of 5-MeO. I'm not like "hey, everybody should try this!" It's incredibly powerful stuff, especially at the dosages that I like to smoke it at, which some people consider dangerous.

Another thing that I'm finding on the west coast, which is spreading everywhere now, is that people really want visions. People have been reading about DMT and ayahuasca and they want to get into this magic zone. There's a lot of want and a lot of expectation. There's a lot of this idea of "I'm a spiritually advanced earth hippy so when I smoke DMT this beautiful thing is going to happen." It's not that easy.

The tryptamines are very strange, shadowy beasts and they open up totally new fields of existence. I think that's the most amazing thing to me. I've come to realize that these realms of consciousness exist and are very real and are around us all the time. The very solidity of my existence seems to have grown less. I believe in my physical existence, but I know that there is much more. So you enter into a different view of the universe.

MB – And it was this realization that gave Robert Augustus Masters absolute terror, rather than experiencing it as liberation. He lives here in Ashland and I've invited him to come talk to me on the show, but he doesn't want to do it. He doesn't even want to talk about 5-MeO. But he's a good example of someone who is presumably spiritually very mature, he'd been practicing yoga and other spiritual disciplines, and he reached a point where he decided, "Well, I want to blow my mind," and that's exactly what he did with 5-MeO.

JO – I think the key there is that you've got to let go. There's a point in the 5-MeO-DMT experience that's all about trust and love and you have to believe that you're going to go to the right place, but you have to let go. I think that parallels can be drawn to the Bardo system with Tibetan Buddhism. You're going to experience this moment of rebirth and you have the choice to move on or go back. 5-MeO-DMT has caused me to totally rethink my ideas about reincarnation. I always used to think that moving on would be the easy bit. I mean, who doesn't want to move on to a higher realm of existence. But you do not know what that realm is going to be like, and you know where you've come from. You know all the things you haven't gotten to do and all the things you'd still like to go back and do. So I suddenly have a very different view and realized that the moment of reincarnation is going to very difficult because there are going to be all these things pulling me back into this life whereas the new life is totally unknown – it's a mystery. So most of us are not going to have belief in the faith and the love and the mystery and give up what we know as reality.

MB – But those are really the rewarding parts of the 5-MeO experience. Certainly I've had my moments with 5-MeO where I've felt, "If I let go at this moment, I'm never coming back," and that's OK. Those are the most powerful experiences. It's about getting out of your own way to experience the fullness of your divinity.

JO – That's when you really experience everything that this has to offer, when you let go of everything that remains of your ego and yourself. It's necessary for the full experience, because your ego can't come along for the ride anyway. It has to be left behind. It's not structured for that dimension.

But getting back to Robert Augustus Masters, reading his account, I feel that when he reached that point, he couldn't let go. He'd done so much training in *vipassana* and all these other practices, that he had actually built up a framework with his ego that allowed him not to let go. He hung on and he hung on and he never let go, so all he experienced was the fear. He went to Stanislav Grof about his experience, and Grof's advice was that he needed to reach full catharsis, even if it meant having people hold him down. He couldn't accept that advice. He couldn't take the experience the whole way.

So from reading his experience, and I go into this in my appendix, I feel like he got himself trapped in it and it was actually, ironically, his training in meditation and all the things he'd done all those years, that created a framework so powerful that he could actually hang onto himself. I've seen that happen with other people who have smoked rather large doses of 5-MeO, but they've managed to stay very grounded and have had to work very hard for it.

One of the reasons that I smoke it alone, mostly now, is I find it annoying when I come out of it. As soon as a come out of the resonant state and I flop back to my ego state, my ego tries to latch onto anything it can find. So, if one of my best friends is sitting beside me and we'd gone climbing together in Pakistan, I'm like, "Oh, wasn't that trip amazing!" or if there's a girlfriend there, I start talking about sex or whatever, because my ego is trying to find anything to relate to. So I'm lying on the ground and everyone is standing around saying "relax and go back into it," and my reaction is "take that shit and bury it in a hole in the desert and never let me touch it again! If you love me, don't ever let me try it again." And of course everybody laughs and says, "we'll hear from you again in about another six months." It's only about twice a year that I can do it now. Another thing is it's only increased in the experience, but the amount I do has actually decreased. I smoke less and less every time, but I can attain the same resonant state just as easily, which is completely against any drug addiction where you need more and more to get back to the same place. With 5-MeO-DMT, it actually seems like I need less and less. It's really bizarre.

MB – For myself, I've reached the point where I have spontaneous 5-MeO experiences where I haven't ingested any medicine at all, but all of a sudden it's like "OK, here I go. Time to relax because it's about to unfold."

JO – I've actually reached the same state with other entheogens now.

MB – Yes, I've experienced the same thing.

JO – Entheogens that never took me there before can now do so. Once again, I think it's this concept of the Bose-Einstein condensate in your brain. Once you've established a pattern and your consciousness can get back into that pattern, it can snap back into it quite easily. I think that that's how shamanism works. Shamans establish a powerful Bose-Einstein condensate in their own minds and if you come in contact with that Bose-Einstein condensate, your mind wants to click into the same pattern. It's like if you meet the Dalai Lama or some highly evolved individuals, I'm always tongue tied – somehow I've got nothing to say. And I feel that my whole consciousness is shifting into this calmer, clearer place, and it's simply from being near a master. The Tibetans have talked about this for years and I think it works.

We've all had the experience with the crazy girlfriend or boyfriend who we dated for a couple months and everything was really good and we couldn't understand all the stories about how crazy they were. It's like your Bose-Einstein condensate is powerful enough to influence their Bose-Einstein condensate and pull them into a more coherent sphere, and then as soon as you separate, they go back to being just as crazy as they were before and you think, "Wow – I never saw that behavior." Sometimes, if a field of energy is strong enough, it can influence other fields of energy around it. That's the whole idea that a truly powerful Bose-Einstein condensate can influence all the fields around it to form the same coherent pattern. I think that this is a key to a lot of this.

MB – Right, in terms of establishing resonant patterns between people. I like to avoid any idea of collective consciousness . . .

JO – I think that collective consciousness is a valid concept and it's related to this akashic field. I think Jung was right on it. He identified where so many of these things come out of. I read a lot of Stanislav Grof. I think he's one of the most interesting cats around, and he does all of the holotropic breathwork. He's administered over 60,000 psychedelic or holotropic sessions, and he's said that traditionally in mysticism, your mysticism is contained within the tradition you grew up in. So Zen practitioners have Zen experiences, and Christian mystics have Christian experiences, Sufi mystics have Islamic experiences. But what's happened in the past 20 years is they're noticing that people having holotropic breath work sessions or entheogenic sessions all over the world are now encountering deities from other religions, and ones that they don't even know about.

There's a story about Stan Groff doing an acid session way back and he encountered this African god and he described it to Joseph Campbell, and Campbell was able to identify which god he saw and which culture it came from. I believe that the amount of consciousness on the planet has increased. Let's not forget that we've doubled the population on the planet in 40 years, so we've doubled the conscious energy on the planet. And it's now so abundant that we really are achieving a global consciousness, and all these ideas and experiences are crossing cultures because the pool is getting so packed.

It's like pottery. Archeologists know that pottery appeared around the planet in several different places at pretty much the same time. Now how can one idea jump from continent to continent? It can't. Obviously someone didn't travel from Africa to South American and tell them how to make a kiln, but if those ideas are flying around in what is now call the noosphere, a term I really like from Wade Davis, which is the collection of all our culture and ideas. The noosphere is now so powerful that ideas can jump from one culture to another or one continent to another. We don't need a physical pipeline. There's a field of energy where all these ideas can move around. I find that concept fascinating.

MB – I find that concept fascinating as well. Personally, I prefer, linguistically, as I mentioned earlier, to cut out the conceptual middle-man. Rather than talk about a collective unconscious or a noonsphere, I just like to call that the Mind of God or the Divine Imagination, and we can all participate in that. Certainly these ideas are there and no, they don't need a physical transmission from one person to another as we can tap into that source and experience that and then we can resonate together culturally or individually. So it's a linguistic parsing that I'm interested in. Since we're all really talking about the same thing, let's just call it God.

JO – I tend to identify the noonsphere with human culture, a layer of the Mind of God if you like. But what is important is that we recognize the fact that the underlying field of energy and information exists. Scientifically it's been proven. One of the things that really amazed me when I started reading Ervin Lazlo's books about the akashic field is that he believes that the entheogenic experience originates within it. He actually states this in one of his books. Since this had been one of my own 'original' ideas, and since I had no idea that Laszlo had given the entheogenic experience any thought at all, I was surprised to say the least! I asked Stan Groff that question in Basil. I asked him if he believed that these experiences originated in from within this akashic field, or zero-point field, whatever you want to call it, and he said that yes, this is where he believed these experiences come from. So scientists and others are considering this to be very possible, and not just entheogen users like myself.

MB – I was just reading the other week about a scientist taking a new perspective of what he called the "biocentric" view because there are all these strange interactions between consciousness and matter and we can't really talk about an objective world outside of our conscious participation in it. His view was that we have to account for how our experience of the physical world relates to consciousness. We can't just talk about objects outside of our perception and experience of them. I see that as really pointing towards the same thing that we're talking about here, that consciousness is involved with this fundamental, underlying energy from which everything emanates out of.

JO – Well let's not forget that there have been two main views, historically, of our existence. One is that matter is primary and that consciousness is an epiphenomenon, and the other is that consciousness is primary and matter is an epiphenomenon, which is the Hindu and Buddhist view that everything is consciousness and the physical world comes out of that. Our Western view for the past 400 years has been that everything is matter, and consciousness is just this annoying and problematic byproduct. I think that paradigm is crumbling rapidly, and many of today's top-of-the-line scientists are now looking for a model that integrates consciousness with the material world, and that is what we're searching for.

At the end of his life, Joseph Campbell was expanding this idea that the body is a bio-energetic field-maker and that all our organs create fields. All the electric fields that everything is generating create the overall field of our experience. It's really fascinating, this idea of the body as a little field-generator. I really like that. And I believe we are entering a paradigm where science will start to recognize everything as fields rather than as particles ... a fundamental shift from the primacy of matter to the realization that the Universe is a conglomeration of energetic fields.

MB – I like that as well. I think that it's really necessary at this point in time to change this paradigm of materiality and consciousness because we've now reached this point where we have a very sophisticated understanding of physical and biological processes in the human body, but as we talked about earlier, we can't actually pinpoint anywhere in the body that consciousness is generated. It seems to just exist on its own. It's not made by anything physical. Understanding fields of energy could be the key to resolving this question.

JO – We're not going to find it in Newton's universe, which is why the quantum paradigm is now really evolving. Unfortunately, 95% of today's scientists were brought up in and believe in the past paradigm, so it's very hard for them to change. For example, Richard Dawkin's book, *The God Delusion*, is every popular at the moment. I found it unreadable. I just couldn't believe how bigoted and narrow-minded his concept of what he wanted to call God was. To him, God was this Judeo-Christian guy that sat up on a throne. To him, that was God and that was ridiculous. He wasn't prepared to expand his view of God to account for modern thinking.

I also read Bernard Hasch, who's a NASA astrophysicist and very much involved in the zero-point energy field. He's written a book called *The God Theory*, which is a marvelous view of how God can fit into current scientific knowledge. His book has probably sold hardly any copies, and I know that Dawkins' book has sold millions of copies worldwide, so I think that's a clear indicator of where we are at. 95% of scientists would like to cut God out of the picture.

But there's so much going on in science at the moment, especially with cosmology, and a part of it is from our super-computers and our space-based telescopes. You've got to remember that in the past 10 –15 years we have significantly increased the amount of knowledge on this planet unbelievably and we're still crunching the numbers. The amount of data is so far ahead of our interpretation of it. We're living in a time of exponential rates of change and we're used to it, because we were born into it. But if you look at it through history or geological time or astronomical time, it's really mind-boggling. I think we don't consider that fact enough.

MB – I think that as these different sciences develop, there will be more and more of a place for God and consciousness. I think that people like Dawkins, this new sort of angry atheist that's out there, are dealing with a caricature of God and dismissing it. That's fine. If you want to dismiss the idea that God is up on his throne and then we look at the religions in terms of their mythology, which is obviously fantasy-based that doesn't really have any grounding in reality . . .

JO – But even that term is wrong; "fantasy-based." What we have are cultural interpretations of God. You were mentioning language before. There's this amazing vanishing languages program that Wade Davis is doing over at National Geographic. We're losing over a language a day in the world. Every time a language is lost, we're losing an entire set of human thought that we have developed over millennium that is a relationship with our planet and our God. When we lose a language we lose a whole way of looking at things. I think that all the visions we have of the Godhead are our cultural ability to recognize God. I really agree with the Hindu concept of Brahma

where the true God, Brahma is sitting on the edge of the universe
with his back turned on us contemplating his god. Whatever God is,
it's a lot more than us, and all we can ever really achieve is our ability
to recognize it. So every god that's ever existed is that culture's
ability to tap into that energy for itself, and that should be progressive
as well. That's one of the main problems with Western culture.
We're holding onto an idea of God that's 2,000 years old and many
religious ideas that have long-since been discounted. These are not
facts. These are metaphors for the revelation of deeper truths. What
we need to be doing is developing a new metaphor – a Quantum view
of God – that can work as a vehicle of transformation and realization
for modern times.

*MB – What the atheists like Dawkins are doing is they're just looking
at these metaphors or those images that no longer work according to
our modern understanding and then dismissing the whole thing,
saying, "Well obviously all of this is just garbage," but they're not
actually looking at the mystical experience. Where does all of this
imagery and poetic language and metaphor come from? What is that
experience? That's what they're not looking at. They're looking at
things like people who believe in the literal interpretation of the Bible
saying that the earth is only 6,000 years old, and since that's
obviously not true, it must all be wrong so they throw it all out. But
the mystical experience doesn't say that the earth is 6,000 years old.
The mystical experience says that God is an actual presence in the
universe and this is something that we can experience. That pulls the
concept of God out of the stories that are told by religion and brings
it back into direct personal experience. I think that Richard Dawkins
would probably write a very different book if he had an opportunity to
try 5-MeO-DMT, for example.*

JO – I'm certainly curious! The bit in *The God Delusion* where he
starts going on about Einstein and other physicists, and how they
shouldn't be talking about their metaphysical visions of God and that
they're doing some kind of damage. What? Albert Einstein isn't
allowed to evolve his concept of what God is? I mean, give me a
break!

MB – It's just the desire to remove the concept of God from our language all together. It's the mistaken notion that we can "just be rational" and we don't need people like Einstein to talk about his mystical inspiration.

JO – Meanwhile, today's cosmologists can get up and say that they believe that moment's before the Big Bang, the matter of the entire universe was concentrated into something about the size of an atom. We're supposed to accept that as being believable, but we can't believe in God? Seems to me like it's all a matter of perspective.

And the discoveries of modern physics and cosmology are so astonishing that to me they bring back these ideas. Like with David Bohm, there has to be an implicate order. There has to be an organization or an intelligence or something. If this universe developed entirely by chance, to me that would be more unbelievable than the existence of an implicate order.

MB – It's just unfathomable that all of this wonderful reality and universe and our very lives and existence is just a random by-product that was produced by chance. That's a leap of faith, actually, to believe something like that.

JO – Richard Dawkins and John Hannah would tell me that because it is, it is. That's the proof. The universe developed this way because that's the only way it could develop. I can understand that point of view, but I find that hard to believe. But once again, it comes back to the experience that is accessible with things like 5-MeO-DMT, of touching the Godhead, that now has made me unable to accept that theory. I have experiential truth, I believe. And Bernard Hasch says the same thing in *The God Theory*. There's no proof for the big bang, but mystics have been recounting the existence of God for millennium. So if we take the accounts of mystics that are very similar – surely that means something. Science has been ignoring them for a long time now.

MB – I think that this is really important to emphasize, especially when we are dealing with the experience. Later, there are all kinds of interpretations and experiences are fit within doctrines and mythological systems and symbol systems, but when we get to the heart of the experience, pretty much everyone seems to be saying things that are very similar, if not identical. That's really important.

JO – Yes. Phenomenologically, they are similar: a void that somehow contains everything, and is conscious.

MB – And if you have a hard time imagining what that would look like, well, 5-MeO-DMT can help you.

JO – Sometimes.

MB – Yes, sometimes.
    Well thank you for sharing with us. It's been a pleasure to speak with you. Your book is out now?

JO – Yes. The book is *Tryptamine Palace* and it's published by Inner Traditions. I want to thank you for this opportunity Martin, and I would like to say one final thing. God Consciousness is real, and is within the grasp of every human being. It is the ultimate realization of being human, and getting more people in touch with this very real source of energy that has been around since the beginning of human time at least, may be the only chance we have of reinventing our society into a ecologically balanced one that can survive the next 50 years.
    If you have already experienced God Consciousness thru 5-MeO-DMT, or other entheogens, or other mystical practices, then know you are being called up. This is our time: we are the sharpened spearhead of humanity, and its up to us to write the future, and lead our tribes out of this fog of extinction denial that our society is choking in, and toward a better future illuminated by the light and love of a universal, transcendental God. Anything less than this is denying the responsibility that is being gifted to us. For as Carl Jung wrote in an essay titled *The Spiritual Problem of Modern Man*, "A higher level of consciousness is like a burden of guilt." Well, the party's over now, so it's time to roll up our shirt-sleeves and get to work. Obviously it's going to take a lot more than just smoking tryptamines to achieve that, but hopefully powerful entheogens like 5-MeO-DMT will prove to be agents for a massive world-wide wake-up call from God. Because the alternative – extinction - is really too sad

to contemplate, and human consciousness, this great experiment, will have been a failure on this planet at least.

VOYAGING TO DMT SPACE

An entheologue with

Dr. Rick Strassman, M.D.

Dr. Rick Strassman, pioneering psychedelic researcher and author of the book, *DMT – The Spirit Molecule*, discusses his new book, *Inner Paths to Outer Space: Journeys to Alien Worlds through Psychedelics and Other Spiritual Technologies*, Zen Buddhism, psychedelics and spirituality, Old Testament prophecy and more in this fascinating interview. Dr. Strassman conducted the first federally approved psychedelic research in the US in nearly a generation with the compound dimethyltryptamine, or DMT, in New Mexico in the mid 1990's. Though expecting mystical raptures and deep psychological insights, in his study he was astonished to find many of his volunteers reporting unexpected encounters with strange and sometimes disturbing alien beings with advanced technology in what amounted to classical UFO "abduction" experiences. Unable to explain away the volunteers' experiences, he concluded that these were genuine encounters with independent sentient beings in otherwise normally invisible dimensions.

For this interview, I visited with Dr. Strassman in his home in Arroyo Hondo, New Mexico, where he currently works in a clinic for psychiatric medicine and is busy laying the foundation for his new research facility, the Cottonwood Research Foundation, where he plans to do continued research on psychedelics and their relationship to spiritual experience, creativity, and higher states of awareness and perception. More information on Cottonwood can be found at www.cottonwoodresearch.org.

Martin Ball – It's a great pleasure to meet you and come out here and do this interview with you. Your new book just came out, Inner Paths to Outer Space. *Maybe you could start by telling us a little bit about it.*

Rick Strassman – Sure. It's a multi-authored book, non-fiction. It's pretty much the brain-child of the second author, whose name is Slavic Wojtowicz, who is an oncology researcher for a pharmaceutical company in New Jersey, and who also happens to be a big science fiction buff and illustrator. He read my book, *DMT: The Spirit Molecule,* and felt that there was a lot of overlap between the material we presented there and the kinds of things that people read and write about in science fiction. He felt it would be a fun and helpful thing to educate people in the science-fiction community about some of these overlaps and areas of similar interests.

He asked me if I'd like to collaborate with him, and I agreed. I asked another colleague of mine, Louis Eduardo Luna, who is a South American anthropologist who divides his time between Brazil and Helsinki and has been working with Ayahuasca for a few decades now. He has probably got one of the more balanced and sophisticated overviews of how to look at and apply the states and plant wisdom information that is associated with Ayahuasca. And so Louis Eduardo agreed to collaborate, and then Louis had a friend in Budapest Hungary named Ede Frecska, who is a Hungarian psychiatrist and has written a lot on new science views on shamanism – having to do with quantum mechanics and non-local theories of information transfer and storage – and so Louis Eduardo asked Ede if he'd like to collaborate. So that's how the four of us came together to collaborate on writing the book.

Each of us contributes three or four chapters. I wrote an overview chapter on psychedelics and DMT and also describe some of the range of experiences that occurred during our research on DMT. My last chapter in the book is probably the one I'm most proud of, which is a fairly long and involved chapter on getting ready for the journey – kind of how one prepares to take a psychedelic trip.

Louis Eduardo wrote several chapters on his relationship with Ayahuasca and the way that he supervises Ayahuasca sessions and Ede Frecska wrote some chapters on shamanism and new scientific paradigms of consciousness through which he explains some of the findings in shamanism. And Slawek wrote some chapters pointing out the commonalities between the material in science fiction books and films with the material that is more well known within the psychedelic community.

MB – Something that comes up time and time again in people's experiences in your book, DMT – The Spirit Molecule, *is that when volunteers are being injected with DMT, they experience UFO's, alternate technologies, and really sci-fi kind of material, so I can see how that would definitely speak to people who are interested in science fiction. Maybe you can tell us a little bit about what those kinds of experiences were like for people and what they were encountering.*

RS – I may want to preface my description of some of those kinds of encounters by stating at the outset neither I nor the volunteers expected anything like the frequency of those kinds of experiences to occur which actually did take place. Both myself and the volunteers were expecting mystical experiences, near death experiences, psychological breakthroughs, those kinds of things.

Now, I was doing my studies in the early 1990's and there may have been a fair amount out there on UFO's and alien abductions, but the volunteers who were in my study weren't that interested in that kind of material and I didn't know much about it and wasn't interested in it either, so I certainly don't think, though one could always argue that it was the case, but I don't think, that it was an example of people expecting to have alien contact sorts of experiences. And Terence McKenna's descriptions of the machines elves and the dwarfs and the pixies hadn't really come out to any extent yet – I don't know if his first book had really come out yet – and not that many people were really familiar with Terence in the early 90's in the first place. So, in that case as well, I don't think it was an example of people's expectations being fueled by their anticipated effects of the drug.

So I think both in terms of more contemporary memes that are passing through our culture, as far as the abduction experience in our culture and Terence's raps, I don't think that either of those had really filtered into the consciousness of our volunteers or my consciousness at the time. So, saying that as an introduction, people were certainly not going into our research studies with hopes of seeing entities or beings. Nevertheless, a huge number of volunteers did. I was reviewing my notes in preparation for writing the DMT book. I completed the research in 95, and sort of did other things for a few years and then returned to my notes, and started writing the book a few years later. I had taken about 1000 pages of notes by the beside of the volunteers – 400 DMT sessions that we gave them over the space of about 5 years – and in reviewing people's accounts of their experiences, probably half, maybe more, reported having the experience of being in some sort of contact, some sort of relationship, more or less passive, more or less active, with these free standing, discretely demarcated, sentient sort of beings. I ended up calling them "beings" rather than "entities" or "aliens" or any of that sort of thing because it seemed like the most neutral term to use, but they were described in various shapes and forms and guises. Sometimes they were humanoid, sometimes they were insectoid, sometimes they were reptilian, and sometimes plant-like. They were more or less aware of the volunteers. Oftentimes they seemed to be expecting the volunteers and were glad to see them, and then began interacting with them.

Other times they seemed surprised and angry that the volunteers' consciousness, at the very least, had intruded upon the sphere of activity of that particular being. Sometimes the volunteers were treated or experimented on. Sometimes they experienced some type of sexual intercourse with the beings. Some were told scenarios of the future. Others were marked somehow or another for future reference in a way. Others showered light and love onto them. Others were guides to lead them to some other place, like through a tunnel leading to a typical near death or mystical experience. So it was the whole gamut of what you might expect.

Some of the motifs were pretty classical science fiction – kind of flying toward a space station or a space ship, or automatons or robots were busily doing their business. Sometimes they would see very hard to describe hybrid entities – machine/animal, even furniture kinds of conglomerates of beings. So, it was one of those things – in giving DMT, it starts very fast, within a few heartbeats, and is over within 30 minutes or so. One of the advantages of a short acting agent like that is you can write down everything that happens in the course of somebody's experience. I wrote down every possible thing

I could – every thought I was having, everything the person was doing and saying, how they looked, the noises in the hall or outside, the emotional ambiance of the ward at the time. So I took a lot of notes and basically, once I wrote the notes and had them transcribed by my secretary, I really stopped thinking about people's individual sessions. So it wasn't until some years later that it really sank in how often indeed people were having those experiences.

MB – And when they're having these experiences, I'm wondering what their physical natures are like. Are they lying down, moving around, are they active, perhaps even acting out some of the situations they're going through?

RS – Well, most people, when they get a big dose of IV DMT are just lying down, and in our study, they are kind of hooked up to machines and IV tubes and a blood pressure cuff and a rectal temperature monitor and all kinds of things like that, so even if they could have moved around, they wouldn't have been able to just because of the physical restraints they were laboring under. But even if they weren't as constrained, a big dose of DMT, even when you smoke it, is pretty disabling, and they just are lying there. People might start to have a tremor or shiver, but any more formed, articulated, purposeful movements were not really that common. So they were just lying there and within 15 – 20 minutes they would start to talk to me and relate what they had just undergone.

DMT extracted from *Mimosa hostilis*. Approximately one dose, vaporized.

MB – Something that I noticed in your book is that many people felt that there would be a point where they had kind of left that aspect of their experience and then returned. Perhaps the DMT is still affecting them, but they feel that they are back in the room at this point. Did you find that people had pretty clear distinctions and transitions between feeling that they are fully in another reality, interacting with these beings and then kind of finding themselves back in the room, back with you, where they could then communicate more freely about what's going on with them?

RS – Well, in our first study, when we just getting the kinks worked out of the protocol, a lot of times people would open up their eyes as the drug was first starting to affect them. First of all, that was pretty startling and disorienting and actually pretty unpleasant as we were doing the study in a pretty standard clinical research type of environment. It was a hospital room with all the accoutrements one would expect. But beside the disorienting aspect of the actual environment itself, it was also confusing too because the visions that the people were having would be overlaid on the objective physical reality of the room at the same time. So it was just a lot easier to monitor what they were experiencing by closing their eyes and not being distracted by the room so that the feeling of the being in the room wasn't as impressive. Within a few months it was obvious that we needed to help people keep their eyes closed because it was just kind of a reflex to open your eyes when you're just so stunned by the onset of effects. So we just got a pair of Wallgreen's eyeshades – the ones you use to sleep during the day time – so even if people did open up their eyes, they would see it was black "outside," so to speak, and just close their eyes again.

The peak of IV DMT occurs within 2-3 minutes of the injection and they start resolving pretty soon after that – so most people could open up their eyes and see me pretty clearly at the 15 minute to 18 minute point, but they'd still be pretty high, and even though they would be pretty eager and quite excited to describe what it was they had just experienced, I encouraged them to keep their eyes closed for another 10 or 15 minutes because there could still be some pretty interesting psychological or maybe emotional material that they could process during that time. And then when they'd open up their eyes again at maybe the half hour point, they were pretty much feeling normal and the visual and emotional effects had pretty much worn off. And that actually corresponded with the blood levels of DMT that we were monitoring all throughout the study. The highest concentrations of DMT occurred within 2-3 minutes after the injection and they'd be negligible or completely gone within 30 minutes and there wouldn't be any at the hour point after the injection.

N,N-DMT

DMT, dubbed "The Spirit Molecule" by Dr. Strassman

MB – Now, in your book, you kind of went out on a limb a little bit in really processing your own surprise with so many encounters with beings, where you write about tuning into, I think you call it, "channel dark matter," in proposing that people seem to be perceiving things not just within their own subjective consciousness, but perhaps perceiving other aspects of reality. I was wondering if you have any additional thoughts on that now, some years later from the study.

RS – It was obviously hard to come up with a model, at least in my mind, at least with what I knew at the time, to really be able to accept and hold and take the stories that people were telling me, and come up with a theory that I could live with scientifically and personally and ones that would make sense to the volunteers.

   I'm a clinical psychiatrist. I learned clinical analysis and how to prescribe anti-psychotic medications, so in terms of the kinds of models that I cut my teeth on as a psychiatric trainee and subsequently, there were primarily biological models and psycho-analytic sorts of Freudian psychology models. In the meantime I had undergone a fairly extensive Zen training and study, which I felt, or thought at the time, gave me a pretty firm understanding or spiritual basis for understanding the psychedelic experience. In fact, the questionnaire that we developed to monitor and rate people's experiences psychologically in DMT was derived from Buddhist psychological principles, so I felt I was pretty well saturated and marinated with Zen Buddhist ideas – including their cosmology of deities and spirits and angels and demons and bodhisattvas and those kinds of things – so I was expecting that I would be able to articulate a theory that would make sense to both me and our volunteers for all the possible varieties of the DMT experience that they might encounter. I just stared off with the most gross explanations and worked up from there when those got rejected. The grossest explanation is obviously that of the brain – this is your brain on drugs – you give people DMT their brain does this – this is why people where having these entity contact experiences.

But every explanation that I tried fell on fairly much deaf ears on the part of the volunteers. They either rejected the ideas about this being a brain on drugs, or the other approach that I was taking that was pretty much a psychological approach – these were unexpressed dreams or impulses or drives or motivations to be special or to belong or to have exciting experiences – kind of the Freudian approach. So when that didn't work, I tried to learn as much as I could as fast as I could, in terms of what Jung had said about UFOs and aliens, so I tried using those models or explanatory systems to kind of encompass people's experiences. That didn't work. I tried the more generic approach of interpreting what they were experiencing as dreams, but that didn't work either.

The idea of the dream state and the DMT state deserves a little bit of thinking about. I think that one of our volunteers summarized it in a succinct and cogent manner when he said that in dreams, you have a dream and then another dream and then another dream, and you kind of pick up with the following dream where the last dream left off. But with the DMT state, as he described it, that level of existence was going on all the while, even when you weren't in it, and you were just kind of dipping into it at the point where it was just happening. If it was a month between trip to trip, then a month of time, in some form or another, had elapsed in the DMT realms, and you were just dipping into it, at the point at which the DMT state was, not necessarily your state, if that makes sense. It's kind of like going to India. It isn't as if you've been to India in January and then returned in June, it wouldn't be that things would begin for you just as they were when you left in January. It's more that you're back in India in June and all this stuff is happening over those five or six months. So that was, I thought, a pretty clear and insightful way of differentiating between dreams and the DMT realm – especially when you enter the DMT state over a week or a space of time, either weeks or months or years.

Also, from the Buddhist point of view, even though I knew a lot the Buddhist cosmology and their worldview, especially with respect to spiritual kinds of realities, either for my own reasons that I never quite swallowed the whole Buddhist rap hook line and sinker, or maybe because it was a Zen community and they were more focused on everyday, here and now reality – chopping wood, carrying water – that I just wasn't feeling that equipped to deal with people's experiences through the lens of Zen Buddhism.

So, I think what the major contribution of my Zen practice was, at the time, to just be as open as I could and to focus more on the immediate situation than being stuck in any kind of theoretical rut that would prevent me from being able to take into account the full impact and depth and variety of what people were experiencing.

I tried and discarded various levels of interpretation until I finally just figured I'll just start to do an experiment assuming that what people are undergoing is real and that indeed they are experiencing or making contact with real, externally verifiable, discrete, freestanding sorts of beings. This is what they're saying and this is what they're doing and this is what is going on between them and the volunteer.

What happened as a result of that is that people became a lot more comfortable in sharing with me the full range of their experiences. I stopped fighting and trying to pigeonhole a peg into a square hole – trying to fit their experiences with the theoretical constructs that I was stuck with. I think as a result of my change in attitude or approach that I was getting deeper and richer reports from people about what was going on. But still, as a scientist, I'm into mechanisms of action and when I started to write the book, I started to hunt around for scientific models that might encompass free-standing, sentient, independently existing, outside just one's mind, explanations for what people were undergoing.

So even though I'm no expert on quantum physics or any of the more far-out psychedelic views of cosmology, I did learn a little bit of this phenomena that is known as dark matter, which is non-visible matter that neither generates light nor reflects light, but still makes up 95% or more of the mass of the universe. It seemed to me that if it makes up that much mass of the universe, it could very well be inhabited, and it would just be a question of changing the receiving characteristics of consciousness through chemical changes that occurred with DMT to be able to perceive things that were normally not perceivable. And there are plenty of examples of that in everyday reality – I mean, with a microscope we can see tiny things we couldn't see normally – with a telescope we can see things very far away we can't see normally, with ultraviolet sensors we can see things that we can't normally see – so the only difference, maybe from a philosophical point of view, is that the change in our receiving powers are not tied in with a machine – they're more in our subjective/receptive consciousness rather than with a piece of metal and electricity and glass and things that can magnify or somehow change the things that we're capable of seeing.

So it's a bit of a stretch, but I don't think it's completely that crazy. The main thing that prevents further movement along the model that I'm talking about is just the verifiability between two people – like can two people see the same thing at the same time – like if you have two people looking through the same microscope at the same time, they can pretty much see and describe the same thing – but is it possible for two people to take DMT at the same time, or not even at the same time, and be able to see the exact same thing?

There are all kinds of caveats about how one would do an experiment like that – especially if there is a wide range of DMT related states, if it's not just one state. I think a lot of what people perceive is based on their own consciousness – their instrument of perception – so if they're depressed or tired or if they're in a good mood or over-energized, didn't get as much sleep as they normally do, or got more sleep than they normally do, I think all of those things will factor into affecting where they will go on any particular DMT experience.

One interesting historical footnote is that when people were first studying Ayahuasca, which is a brew from the Amazon that contains DMT and also another plant that has a substance in it that allows the DMT to be orally active - otherwise when you just swallow DMT it's broken down – but the Amazonian Indians discovered that if you combine a DMT containing plant with another plant which contains an enzyme inhibitor that the oral DMT then becomes active – when chemist were first looking at the chemical composition of Ayahuasca, one of the compounds that they isolated they named telepathine, which I think was a reflection of how commonly it is reported by South American natives that they share perceptual effects when under the influence. And I actually know a couple of Western scientists who were doing some studies down there some time ago and they were in a small circle and they both drank DMT together and they both had the exact same vision of a big bird, like a vulture, sitting just outside the circle, which just the two of them were able to see – no one else did in their group. So I think experiments can be designed that can try to standardize as many of the independent variables as possible to see if people do enter the same state with DMT and other really powerful psychedelic drugs, and if they did, then that would lend some more credibility to the idea that it is something that isn't just one's individual hallucination.

MB – It sounds like part of the difficulty, coming from a Western standpoint, is that we don't really have a sophisticated model of consciousness. We're getting very sophisticated with neurochemistry and neurobiology and looking at brain states in relation to neurons and chemicals and molecules in the brain, but we don't really have a firm model of subjective states of consciousness, and it sounds as if this research could really be paradigm shaking if we can get to performing this at a high level of examining what's really going on.

RS – I think we'd also have to have some models that can incorporate those sorts of experiments and if those findings did come through in the way that I would expect them to, and to interpret those findings.

In this new book, *Inner Paths to Outer Space*, Ede Frecska describes some of the theories that are being circulated regarding non-locality and also some of the network ideas with respect to microtubules, and microfilaments that are contained within the nervous system – so I think we're starting to develop some theoretical models

MB – Coming from quantum biology then . . .

RS – It isn't really coming from within mainstream psychology or psychiatry, it would have to be some kind of hybrid of quantum science and maybe even an introspective science, like some of those that have been developed in introspective traditions that have been around for thousands of years.

It is interesting that in terms of the long span of human history we are one of the few cultures that does not believe in a free-standing spiritual level of reality. We've kind of thrown out anything that can't be objectively measured or imaged or photographed into the waste bin of superstition or supernaturalism, and we've got this view that things that can't be seen by a group of people at the same time are not real – that's a relatively recent development in the long span of human consciousness. That's not necessarily to say that old ideas are true ideas, but the vast majority of humans, for the vast majority of time, have firmly believed in and utilized to the best of their abilities the belief in and the conviction in a free-standing spiritual level of reality.

That could mean that it's a true fact – that there is a non-visible, only subjectively experienced, spiritual level of reality that we're so far ignoring or relegating to unreality. It may be that it's through the tools of science and pharmacology that we are also able to validate non-corporeal levels of reality and we can learn from and interact with the inhabitants there of and maybe get back on course.

MB – So, let's step back in time a little bit and talk about what inspired you to do this DMT study. I think that yours was the first study to be done in something like 30 years for research on psychedelics in the United States, and you write about in your book how this was a very difficult challenge to actually make that happen. So I'm kind of curious about what inspired you to delve into that hornet's nest and also what made you choose DMT as what you wanted to study.

RS – In terms of what got me interested in the whole field in the first place, I went to college in the late 60's and the early 1970's, when there were two very interesting converging lines of research and experience. There was a discussion going on and a whole new level of experience was being had by people and these were, on one hand, the Eastern religious practices and traditions, especially Buddhism and Hinduism, and on the other hand, there was this influx of experiences being brought on by the ingestion of psychedelics. And it didn't escape all that many people's attention that there was a lot of similarity in people's descriptions of those two sets of experiences. So I started thinking to myself, if the descriptions of meditators comport so closely, at least in some respects, with the reports of some people taking psychedelic drugs, then there must be some kind of biological concomitant going on in the brain at the time that people are having deep mystical experiences. So I began to search for a biological basis for mystical experience because it seemed as though there must be as they were so similar.

It seemed like there must be something going on in the brain at the same time that people were having these non-drug induced experiences that might at least in some ways be similar to what happens in the brain in reaction to a psychedelic drug. So I began to hunt around within the literature for a biological basis for mystical experience. I didn't know about DMT at the time – this was in the late 60's – and actually a lot of the research on psychedelics in humans was winding down. But I did learn about the pineal gland, which is a small organ in the center of the brain which had been thought to have a spiritual role to play in the spiritual physiology of the Hindus, in particular in regard to the chakra system. So I started to learn about the pineal. It was a few years later that the whole phenomenon of winter depression became current, and there was an interest in the role of melatonin, which is the main hormone of the pineal gland, which is involved in causing winter depression. So that was actually the root through which I was able to get involved in clinical research regarding my unspoken interest in spiritual states and spiritual consciousness. I ran a study at the university of New Mexico looking at the role and the function of melatonin. And even though it was a pretty psycho-pharmacological kind of study, looking at a whole range of hormones and autonomic functions, my underlying interest was to see if there were any psychedelic effects of melatonin.

So when that came up short, I decided to switch fields and go more directly into the field that I was fundamentally interested in, which was the psychedelic work. I had learned by that time about the existence of DMT as a very powerful psychedelic chemical that exists in plants and animals, including mammals and including humans, and the great amount of interest that DMT had garnered in the psychiatric research field in the 50's and 60's and the early 70's, and so even though there are no data yet connecting the pineal gland with DMT, there is a lot of circumstantial evidence that suggested a relationship between the two things. There were a number of reasons that I chose to begin using DMT, one of which was its possible but still unproven relationship to the pineal. The other is its endogenous nature – it occurs in human beings and I felt it was important to study it carefully and find out more about the effects of a naturally occurring psychedelic. I mean, nobody is looking at this, really, even to this day. It's still kind of a minor substance of abuse, but when you really think about the existence of this incredibly mind-blowing psychedelic that's being made in our bodies at all times by the lungs and the red blood cells and the brain, those sites of formation are fairly well established at this time . . .

Nobody is thinking or really talking about what could be the role of DMT in normal consciousness and in extraordinary states of consciousness. When people first were looking at naturally occurring DMT in humans, they of course were looking at it from the psychiatric point of view. For example, perhaps it causes schizophrenia. And there were a number of studies that compared the levels of DMT in the blood of schizophrenics versus normal people and they really weren't able to find any differences. But the levels of DMT occurring in everyday existence are so low that you really need incredibly sophisticated equipment to make a differentiation between the levels you might find in one group of people compared to the levels you might find in another group of people, so I think those studies suffered from a lack of technological expertise that hopefully we have made some progress in overcoming in the last 20 or 30 years.

In terms of a rationales to study DMT, one of the reasons I presented to the regulatory and funding bodies was that it was important to understand more the effects of externally applied DMT so we could then start to determine the levels of similarities and differences between psychosis and between the state of DMT intoxication that we were expecting to see in our volunteers. The other reason I chose DMT was because it was relatively obscure and it had been a couple of decades at least since anybody in the US had done human studies giving psychedelics to people. I was afraid that if we began our studies giving people a drug like LSD, or even psilocybin, that it would garner a lot more publicity than beginning with a relatively obscure drug like DMT. The other reason we chose DMT was because of its extremely short duration. I was thinking that it would be pretty stressful for our volunteers to being given a psychedelic drug in the hospital and I was suspecting that people would perhaps undergo adverse affects or panic or get pretty disabled or disoriented. I was thinking that it would be much more manageable to deal with a 10 or 20 minute bad trip than a 6-10 hour bad trip.

MB – Something that seems to be a central and reoccurring them that runs through your discussion of a lot of this is really looking at the question of mysticism or spiritual states of consciousness or visionary states of consciousness, and of course you do raise in your book the controversy between what we can consider mainstream religious practitioners who tend to look down on the use of visionary medicines as being authentic spiritual experiences, at least within Western tradition, but certainly you're asking the larger questions of how this relates to spiritual experience. What is your view on that?

RS – It's not any clearer than when I set out on this work. An interesting aspect of my involvement with the Zen community that I was with for over 20 years – I was a lay member – I was never a monk – I was ordained as a lay member and I ran a meditation group that was affiliated with the main temple – I never shaved my head and donned robes though and never got an Asian name, but I went up there fairly regularly, and frequently, and underwent lay ordination and was entrusted with teaching meditation and Zen for a couple of decades. So in the beginning of my relationship with the monastery – I was in my early 20's, as were most of the monks who were there at the time, and every chance I got I would take one of the monks aside and ask them if they had taken LSD, and if they had, how important their LSD experience was in their decision to enter a monastic lifestyle. At the time, this was probably 1974 that I started to spend time at the monastery and be friends with the monks, I'd say at least 3/4, maybe 80-90% of the monks had an LSD experience, and the vast majority of them, probably every one of them, felt that their LSD experience was their first glimpse that there was another way of looking at reality.

In Buddhism, that's what's called *bodhicitta*, which is the thought of enlightenment, which, for a lot of Buddhist thinkers, is the most important step on the road to enlightenment – the realization that enlightenment exists and is possible to experience. So strictly speaking, for almost everyone – 3/4's of the monks at that particular temple who had had an LSD experience – their first entry into the enlightenment stream of life was through an LSD experience. So that validated in a lot of ways my thinking of the similarities and overlap and the relevance of the psychedelic experience to a spiritual lifestyle and a spiritual worldview and a spiritual way of interacting with people and with things.

I described some of the ins and outs of my relationship with the monastery over the years and pretty much as long as I kept the level of discussion and discourse just between me and a monk, and they for sure all chatted together about the laymen and laywomen who had come through for workshops and retreats and made sure that everybody was on track – so I'm sure that they were talking about my interests in psychedelics and the role that they play in spiritual growth. So I got quite a bit of explicit encouragement over the years from these monks who had taken LSD and were climbing the hierarchy of the monastic organization. But it was only when I was actually starting to put the rubber to the road in doing my studies and both speaking and writing publicly about the association between the psychedelic experience the spiritual life and practice that the monastery started getting the jitters and for a number of reasons had to disavow any relationship between the two and any relationship between me and them. So that was a fairly good example of even an Eastern religion, which ostensibly puts more faith in the truth than in orthodoxy or any dogma, being faced with the public relations fallout that might be associated with any linking of their organization and me promulgating psychedelics as a possible way to work on one's spiritual life.

I certainly, at the time, never suggested that psychedelics were a replacement for spiritual practice. On the contrary, I think that one of the things that you can get from the psychedelic experience is a view – a glimpse, and that's what the monks and I had been talking about all these years, was how you got your first glimpse and then you worked on it every day, 24 hours a day. But those kinds of subtle distinctions were lost in the heat of the argument over whether there is a role for psychedelics within Buddhist practice. It was disappointing – it wasn't that surprising. This sort of break with the Buddhist community occurred in 1996 and I haven't really had anything to do with them since. I still do meditate on my black cushion, but I turned in my small piece of cloth that demarcated my membership as a lay Buddhist. I returned that to the mother temple a couple of years after the split.

But as the result – there's always a silver lining – the fact that I lost one religious community forced me to start re-examining my own spiritual roots, which are Jewish in nature. So for the last 10 or 12 years I've embarked on a fairly rigorous course of self-study of Hebrew texts and commentary and scriptures and have found that in a lot of ways they've augmented and filled in a lot of the gaps I had been struggling with in regard to a real spiritual view that could incorporate both a psychedelic experience and a religious experience. So I've been just starting to formulate the ways in which I can describe that in a sense that is intelligible and compatible with a more Western worldview of a more religious and psychedelic sensibility.

I've been circling around the Old Testament idea of the prophetic state of consciousness, which I think in some ways can allow for an incorporation of the psychedelic state – though there are a lot of dissimilarities – but probably more importantly is the information that comes in the psychedelic state. I think one of the pitfalls that the contemporary use of psychedelics is suffering from is that there isn't a culturally relevant framework in which to take home and incorporate the lessons of the psychedelic experience. A lot of it is, "Oh wow! That's the most amazing experience of my life and now I see that all is One," but that isn't really the prophetic viewpoint. The prophetic viewpoint is that there is information that is experienced in these exalted states and so what is that information?

So there's a huge amount of material in the first handful of books of the Hebrew bible, but especially in the prophetic books such as Isaiah and Jeremiah and Ezekiel. A fair number of them underwent incredible psychedelic visions on one hand, and on the other hand they really did a lot of teaching about what they felt and heard and thought and saw under the effect of that altered state of consciousness. And what they bring back isn't all that exalted – ethical teachings and moral teachings and a view of God and of history that isn't especially unique or far-out, but it's quite Western and as a result, it takes a lot of swallowing of bitter pills by most Westerners to get past their visceral aversion to looking at the Bible as a sacred text. There are probably more people in the psychedelic community that have read the *Bhagavad Gita* and the Buddhist sutras than have read the Bible. And that's cool, but it's kind of crazy too because the answers to how you incorporate and how you live under the umbrella of a psychedelic worldview or through a lens that's compatible with our Western worldview is kind of right beneath our noses.

It's a powerful book, obviously. Look at the course of world history as it's been driven by this vision of the Bible, especially of the Hebrew bible and all the prophets and Israel as the chosen ones, the Ten Commandments, and the Red Sea and Abraham and all that – you know, there's a tremendous amount of information there that is accessible, though it's pretty dense and it's fairly obfuscated by the efforts of the clergy and the rabbis, as it were. But it's still there, and the first step is to review what's in the Bible as a means of trying to articulate a psychedelic type of vision that is informed in the West. You know, we're not shamans. We didn't spend our infancy and childhood and adolescence and adulthood in the jungle and you know, we're not Buddhists or Asians or Indians or Japanese, we're not Native Americans. We're people who emerged from the matrix of the Bible, more or less.

People talk about a Judeo-Christian worldview, but I think it's more Jewish, because Jewish is the roots from which both Christianity and Islam grew, so I think that's our worldview. And to just reject it out of hand without knowing about it I think is a mistake, because there are quite a number people out there in power, both governmental and other power, who are familiar with what's written in the Bible, and if the psychedelic community is not, I think our ignorance hurts us in a couple of ways. For one, we can't counter some of the crazy, fundamentalistic interpretations of the text, but on the other hand, we aren't able to take advantage of what's there to live a psychedelically informed type of life in a culturally relevant way for us. I don't think that we have to reinvent the wheel, but we do have to return to our origins a little bit more intently, critically and passionately.

MB – So I notice on your bookshelf here, which we are sitting next to, you do have a copy of Magic Mushrooms in Religion and Alchemy *by Clark Heinrich where he talks a little bit in this book about looking at some of the prophets form the Old Testament as actually being mushroom hunters and gathers. He makes an argument for Moses and the Ten Commandments, the burning bush, and looking at all that as actually relating to amanita mushrooms.*

RS- I think those are fairly strong and well-reasoned arguments, but I think rather than looking for some external source of the psychedelic experience, once again we have them under our noses. All of us are always making DMT at all times, so I don't think it's actually necessary to take in something from the outside that will cause the psychedelic experience – we've got the machinery in our brains already. I think even more remarkable than the effects or presence of mushrooms or acacia plants as being responsible for the visions of the prophets, a more prudent explanation, is that there may be some role of naturally occurring DMT or comparable psychedelics as mediating those types of phenomena.

MB – I also wanted to ask if you have any thoughts on the preponderance of DMT in nature. It seems kind of surprising that it is in so many different species of plants and it seems to be everywhere, to some extent, and it's also inside us. Do you think that this is just part of our evolution and our physical bodies developing neurotransmitters and whatnot, that we're taking in these influences from the plants that we might be encountering or eating? It seems kind of odd that we have the chemical both within us and it's in so many plants.

S – I can speculate regarding that, but I think the person who really articulates that vision or some of the ideas behind that even better is Denis McKenna, and actually we've got a really fantastic interview with him for the DMT documentary that's in the works, which I hope will come out, maybe next year, if all goes well. I asked him that exact question – what do you think is going on with DMT being a ubiquitous as it is? I think a simple-minded answer, but one that fits the bill as well as anything, is that the presence of DMT is a shared conduit, in a way. It's the medium through which individuals or species that contain it are able to relate to each other.

It's a fairly common phenomenon when people take DMT, or any strong psychedelic for that matter, that they're able to understand the consciousness of animals and plants too a much greater extent than they ever were before. It isn't quite the case that you take DMT and you understand a rock or a couch or a stove (though some people do). It's a little more common of a phenomenon that people seem to describe a deeper level of empathy and consciousness sharing and communication with particular sorts of animals or plants. So it could be that DMT is the matrix through which we can maybe communicate with other beings that also contain DMT. It wouldn't necessarily be through the spoken language. It would be maybe more telepathic or empathic or visual or visceral, emotional kinds of content, but compelling and real content nonetheless.

MB – I suppose in one sense we can say that it allows for interspecies communication on this level, but on the prophetic level, allows for communication beyond our immediate physical reality as well.

RS – That could be. I think it's really strange that everyone isn't studying DMT. Everybody ought to be studying DMT – I mean, what's going on here? We have this incredibly weird chemical in our brains that seems to allow inter-species communication and seems to allow the reliable and reproducible entry into a spiritual state, it's a naturally occurring chemical – our brains make it, our lungs make it, our red blood cells make it, it lasts a half hour, you can infuse it into people for a few hours at a time and it retains its psychedelic potency, so it's almost like this spigot or valve that you can just turn on and open to some kind of consensus reality and observationally agreed upon way of looking at things or anybody at any time, so that's a question that I think about all the time. Why isn't everybody looking into this? Which you may want to counter with the same question – so why aren't YOU looking at it?

In some ways, that brings us to the end of the book, my DMT book, which if you read between the lines, it was clearly the case that

I was in over my head. I had a tiger by the tail and I might hurt somebody or hurt myself and it was just too complicated, so I took a break. I had to work through things on my personal level, on the level of my spiritual development, and had to go back to the drawing board and reintegrate myself into my Jewish roots and learn about the Bible and the Hebrew language and the prophets and really start to get a handle on what seemed to be a spiritual level of reality – angels, demons, God, the afterlife and non-corporeal levels of existence and the way in which they interact with the physical level of existence – and I also had to make a living.

So it's been 12 years, almost 13 now, that I gave my last dose of anything to anybody. I'm feeling like I'm more in a position to renew the research, so that's why myself and a couple of colleagues put together the Cottonwood Research Foundation in the last year to renew studies with psychedelics, especially the psychedelic plants in a more humane and larger-view perspective of what these plants and drugs are able to provide access to, both in terms of information and their human properties, those kinds of things. We're just getting off the ground. We have a little bit of money in the bank and I'll be taking a vacation for a month or so after I complete my contract at a local clinic here. Then when I return this late summer, I'll be hitting the ground running to try and do some more fundraising and developing some proposals for grants. I'm also collaborating with a group right now up in Seattle trying to get an Ayahuasca study off the ground.

So I think this time around, I want to be helpful rather than clever, which was kind of the approach I was taking with the first series of studies. I was being clever in as much as I wanted to give people DMT and describe its effects and understand the brain chemistry going on behind it, but I was a little too hands-off. I was pretending that I wasn't interested in what the effects were other than just kind of knowing what they were. But I think that it's more important to apply those effects and to be helpful rather than just gaining some information, which was sort of my approach, for lack of a better reason.

But I was constrained by the model though. It was the government and it was a grant for brain chemistry and psychopharmacology and I couldn't have gotten anywhere without using that kind of model, but I opened up the door to get this new wave of American research up and running. But it's been kind of slow, so that's another reason that I opened up the Cottonwood. The pace of psychedelic research in the US has been quite slow since I left the field in '95 and seems as though it can use some re-energizing and reorienting away from the strictly scientific model. Clearly we're not going to be going off the deep end, but we're going to try and enlarge the questions that we try to address using the scientific model. It won't be strictly limited to brain chemistry and psychopharmacology.

MB - Obviously with Ayahuasca it would again be looking at DMT. Is there a reason other than that why you are interested in looking at Ayahuasca?

RS – Well, there's a whole lot of information out there about the effects and properties of Ayahuasca, and the reports that I've been hearing is that it is the mother of all healers, so any I think that any plant that has that kind of reputation is worth studying. Up in this part of the world and in northern New Mexico, there is a huge problem with alcoholism and other substances being abused. There's a couple of centers in Latin America using Ayahuasca to treat substance dependence and there's a slowly increasing number of reports in the scientific literature as well that seem to confirm the impression that lots of substance abusers are able to stop abusing once they've undergone a number of sessions with Ayahuasca, so that's a natural set of studies that would be easy to do and wouldn't be hard to get funding and approval for, just because of the nature the problem is quite so pressing.

And it is DMT, and I like DMT. I made my career out of it, and it's a plant, so it's not quite as harsh an experience. It's a little gentler, someways, than a pure extracted powder that you inject into somebody's veins. There's a tremendous amount of information about Ayahuasca in the non-psychiatric literature – in the anthropological literature and religious literature, indigenous literature and the oral traditions, so I think that it's possible to utilize some of those sources of information that are at least ostensibly external to the scientific worldview, at least at this time in our history.

MB – Of course, recently in the past couple years we did have the study by Johns Hopkins University that looked at psilocybin that, not surprisingly, came back and said that something like 65% of participants described their experience as being deeply mystical, deeply spiritual, and the most significant experiences of their lives. I wondered if you had any thoughts on their study?

RS – It's a great study. It was quite well done and their control situation and actual implementation of the study was impeccable. On the other hand, it was basically a repeat of a comparable study that was done at Harvard University of giving psilocybin to divinity students and a large number of them also described results comparable to the ones that just came out of the Hopkins study. I think in some ways, comparable to the study I was doing with DMT, the Hopkins psilocybin mysticism study was kind of going back to basics, to, number one, establish that you can do these kinds of experiments in a safe manner, and number two, at least in terms of the Hopkins study, that you can induce positively valenced subjective experiences. I think that the next step is to be creative and start to apply some of these potentially beneficial effects in a healing and therapeutic manner.

I understand the Hopkins group is interested in doing some substance abuse work, specifically with psilocybin, so I think the more therapeutic work is done, the better. I think that when you're working in a strictly university setting that your explanatory models are a bit more constrained than if you were working in a free-standing institution like Cottonwood is going to be. I don't think that they'll be quite able to talk about p-values and statistical power in quite the same breath that they can talk about spirits and plants and the natives and angels and helping beings and those kinds of things. We wouldn't be using those terms and models in any of our scientific work, but I think we'll be freer to discuss those explanatory models in our more speculative models of what might be going. In the best of all possible worlds, we'd like to have Cottonwood be an institution of higher learning that kind of revolves around the psychedelic experience. So we would apply every relevant discipline that has an interest in the psychedelic state, which would include anthropology and religion and shamanism, psychology, cognitive sciences, psycho-pharmacology and therapeutics, let alone just from the pure psychiatric point of view.

I think both levels of discourse have to take place. The university is a more appropriate institution for certain levels of discourse, but I think there needs to be a really explicit and overt role of a spiritual worldview in any full discussion of the psychedelic experience and its relevance to growth and healing and creativity. When you're in a university setting, you have to be much more circumspect in those disciplines that you might bring to bear on the discussion.

MB – So it really sounds like you're trying to open up the paradigm here and move it out of the scientific reductionistic model, or at least scientific explanation of things and genuinely acknowledge that, look, there really is something going here that is opening people up to different levels of spiritual experience and perception, whatever that may be, and really is affecting people's lives.

RS – Psychiatry is a relatively recent invention, and these drugs and plants have been used for a long time before there was even a word "psychiatry," so I think that there are other people and cultures that know a lot more about the effects of these plants than we do. To pretend that's not the case or to hold ourselves out as having a more advanced or superior view or any kind of hegemony over the knowledge of what kinds of experiences these kinds of plants can bring on, I think the term is hubris, is a little far fetched that we can't learn from other cultures and traditions that have been around a lot longer than we have and have a lot more experience in the trial and error process of the scientific method using the tools that were and still are at their disposal for using these plants and their effects on our consciousness.

MB – It sounds like this could also potentially have a large impact on culture. For one, from a legal perspective, looking at these scientific studies and things like the UVD or Santo Daime making court cases for their legal right to use Ayahuasca, but could also potentially have broader effects within culture itself, that if we have people like yourself studying the spiritual effects of these plants and visionary medicines, it could perhaps change other people's attitudes and their openness to what the potential of these plants might really be.

RS – I don't think that we're going to come to the answers either through science or through religion. I think it's going to be some kind of hybrid. Science is a bit too constrained in the model building, and most religions are too constrained through the maintenance of their institution at the expense of the truth. As a rule, if you can establish the veracity of your findings through science, it's believed. It isn't excluded necessarily because someone disagrees with your findings. So I think it will require some kind of hybrid of scientific religion or spiritual science to be able to take into account the entire range of the phenomenon, the ethical implications that's available and also maintain the peer review and the cross-checking of your findings that occurs within the scientific model. Yeah – so it's pretty out there. It's kind of a large view and if I get one half of one percent done before I die, I'll feel pretty good about that.

MB – Do you think society is ready for that?

RS – I don't know . . . I'll find out . . . It could be . . . I mean, people are hungry, and they're lost. We're not doing so well as a species. People are taking psychedelics. I think as a means of living their life, science falls pretty short, but as a means of taking into account reality, religion falls pretty short. So I think people are looking, but they don't know quite where to look. If we can begin developing Cottonwood where these things can be looked at carefully and experiments can be designed and explanatory models are offered that take into account the entire range of possibilities of what is going on, then we might make some headway into establishing a new kind of hybrid model.

MB – What can those of us out there in the entheogenic community do to support this kind of work and research, and specifically, what can we do to support the Cottonwood Research Foundation?

RS – If you go onto the website for Cottonwood (www.cottonwoodresearch.org), you'll see the projects that we're beginning to work on, and we'll give you the opportunity to donate, so tell your friends and family and try and spread the word. We need money. Obviously, any research projects take lots of funding and time, and the more time I have to work on things, the more I'll do them. I'll be giving up my clinic job at the end of this summer and after I return from being gone for about a month, I'll be working on Cottonwood more in a bald-faced appeal for my own support. The more money I can bring in for operating expenses, the more time I can devote to Cottonwood.

We don't need much in the way of local volunteers right now. Once we get our coffers a little more plentiful, we'll be able to hire some staff. Ultimately, we're going to need some land, some buildings, some medical staff, a psychiatrist, a nurse, people who are keen on this work and are willing to devote themselves to it, so a few really large grants would help. A lot of small donations would help. It's a very long-range goal. The more funding we get, the more quickly we'll be able to start implementing some things. I have a contractor friend who's beginning to draw up some sketches and designs for the research suite with a couple of research rooms and a lab and a kitchen and a lobby and those kinds of things. Once that's firmed up, I'll be posting those to the web site. It's pretty young and inchoate rate now. I'm a patient person – obviously I wouldn't have gotten my research on DMT done if I weren't – so I've got plenty of time to work on it, and even if I didn't, it's got to be started off in the way that I would like it to turn out.

I think that one of the problems with our University of New Mexico work with DMT was that I felt like it was important to get this work started no matter what it took to get it started in the US and I was willing to do that. But I think as a result of just doing whatever had to be done to get my funding and my permits in order, I kind of painted myself into both a conceptual and practical corner. This time around I don't feel like I have much to prove. I've done the DMT work, I've written a couple of books. I feel as though I've left a good legacy behind. Other people have taken the baton and run their own studies, so I think that in respect to the Cottonwood, I would want to begin it the way that I would ultimately like it to turn out. If it never manifests in that particular way, then that's fine - it's obviously not meant to be at this time. And if we can get the funding to do it in a way that I think it needs to be done and do it right, then great – we'll go ahead and get started.

MB – So in the ideal world, where would you like to start a study on Ayahuasca, if everything could fall into place nicely?

RS – The first thing is to start giving Ayahuasca to people in this country, and that could occur anywhere. There's a group up in Seattle that's beginning that, though it isn't clear how quickly they'll be able to get started. But that could occur here in New Mexico or anywhere in the US, as long as somebody starts giving people Ayahuasca in at least a relatively humane setting. Obviously the more humane and attentive it is to the non-psychiatric aspects of the setting, the better. In terms of the treatment center, the obvious thing I'd like to do, living in New Mexico with the rampant alcoholism and other substance abuse problems we have here, is to have that kind of a protocol locally. But it would need to be in a conducive environment and that's the only way that I would be giving people drugs or psychedelics again, in a compassionate and humane setting.

MB – One last thing that I'd like to touch on is you mentioned in your new co-authored book that you have a chapter that basically gives some advice for those who would personally venture out on this journey. I wondered if you could just touch on a couple of the ideas that you've expressed in there.

RS – I'm quite pleased with that chapter. It's called "Preparing for the Journey." It's a fairly long-range view of getting ready for any kind of psychedelic experience. It takes into account the psychological work and preparation one needs to undergo to establish some kind of discipline, either psychological and/or spiritual to try and understand yourself and your motivations as well as you can. And I do spend a lot of time in that chapter emphasizing the importance of intent – to clarify over and over again what your intent is to undergo a psychedelic experience. The more you know of your intent, the more you'll be able to do the necessarily preliminary work to get the most out of the amplification of your normal mental and spiritual faculties through which these substances work.

For example, if your intent is to work on psychological sorts of issues, if you can spend some time in psychotherapy first with a psychotherapist that you like and you trust and think is helpful. You can do a lot of the legwork that would make it easier to make the most out of your psychedelic experience. And it may even turn out to be the case that you don't need to have the experience if you've gotten what you need out of the psychological work. If you're interested a mystical experience, it's a helpful thing to educate yourself on the literature of mystical states, especially if you can find something within your own tradition, and do some work and study with a master within that tradition. So the preparation can extend for months or even years before the actual trip.

I also discuss some of the more proximate kinds of planning that one can do, such as deciding if you're going to be tripping alone or with a group. If with a group, is there going to be a leader? Are you going to be alone or have someone with you? What kinds of preparations are you going to have in case you get sick or if someone panics or gets confused? Issues of staying nearby, when to drive – those kinds of immediate things that you want to make certain you've looked after. Getting enough sleep, are you feeling healthy? Are you especially stressed out or jet-lagged? Taking care of business like taking out the garbage, even taking care of your will, if you're old and you have some concerns that you may die – which, you know, isn't very common, but it can happen. You certainly can, at some point in a big trip, experience some fear of dying or be convinced that you have died. Taking care of every possible problem that you can anticipate, and making sure that you are steering the trip in anticipation of a good trip to optimize the kinds of effects that you have. And also ancillary instruments such as writing tools or art supplies, those kinds of things. I also spend time at the end of the chapter talking about integration issues and how to deal with adverse effects such as panic, depression, or anxiety, those kinds of things.

MB - And what was the name of the book again?

RS – It's called *Inner Paths to Outer Space*. It's published by Inner Traditions, the same group that did the DMT book and it is on Amazon and Barns and Nobel, and ask your local bookstore to carry it if they don't already.

MB – And it has a beautiful cover. We're very lucky to have the original art piece here in the house that we're able to look at and it really is fantastic. I'm looking forward to seeing what else is in the book – it looks like a very good one.
    Thank you very much for your time.

RS – You're very welcome. I hope it was helpful.

GORDON WASSON, JOHN ALLEGRO AND THE HOLY MUSHROOM

An Entheologue with

Jan Irvin

Jan Irvin is an independent researcher, author and lecturer. He is the author of the new book *The Holy Mushroom: Evidence of Mushrooms in Judeo-Christianity*, 2008, and is the co-author of the book *Astrotheology & Shamanism: Christianity's Pagan Roots*, 2006/2009, and co-producer of the DVD *The Pharmacratic Inquisition*, 2007, with Andrew Rutajit. Jan Irvin is also the curator of the official website for John Marco Allegro, the much-criticized Dead Sea Scrolls scholar, and has contributed much to the re-examination of many of Allegro's theories. For more information on Irvin's work, visit www.gnosticmedia.com and for more on Allegro, visit www.johnallegro.org.

Martin Ball – Welcome to the Entheogenic Evolution.

Jan Irvin – Thank you, Martin, for having me on.

MB – I wondered if you could first tell us a little bit about yourself and how you got into the work that you're doing with Gnostic Media

JI – Let me see if I can give you the short version here. Basically, I met Jack Herer in December of 1992 and worked with him for a while on the California Hemp Initiative. During that time he turned me onto a book by John Marco Allegro called *The Sacred Mushroom and the Cross*. Allegro was one of the original translators of the Dead Sea Scrolls and came out in 1970 with this book stating that Christianity was based on a fertility drug mushroom cult. Jack had spent a lot of his time in the 80's researching the leads in Allegro's book and he was adamant, against the views of a lot of other scholars out there, that Allegro's correlations were correct. At first I thought some of the ideas that he proposed sounded pretty strange and then when I started thinking about it over the years I started realizing that actually a lot of his ideas, as Clark Heinrich mentions in his book as well, were a lot more reasonable than many of the literal interpretations that we accept for the major religions today.

MB – It sounds like Jack Herer was something of a mentor for you.

JI – Yeah. We're still good friends after all this time. We still talk and share research. Certainly, at one point, probably about ten years ago, I branched off and started doing a lot of research on my own. Jack didn't even know that I had done all that research when I came back to him and he would tell me things and I'd say, "Yeah, I know!" So at one point we started clicking on the research. And then in 2003 I met Andrew Rutajit, my co-author for the first book, *Astrotheology & Shamanism*, and he had started the Gnostic Media project. We started using that as a mutual website for the book and the DVD, *The Pharmacratic Inquisition*. Eventually, times changed and I ended up buying 100% of Gnostic Media. So that's how I ended up with it, but I've been working with Gnostic Media since 2003. In terms of all the projects that are on there now, I am a core part of them.

MB – So you've been pretty busy in building up Gnostic Media and doing your research. It sounds like it was a personal research program for you. You got into this and decided that you were going to pursue this in depth?

JI – Exactly. I guess what really got me started was that Jack Herer had a $10,000 challenge on the back of his book, *The Emperor Wears No Clothes*, to disprove his claims about hemp.

MB – Has anyone cashed in on that?

JR – No. And now it's up to $100,000. When I was eighteen/nineteen years old, I thought that was a lot of money (the $10,000), so I started reading a lot of books and after a couple of years I realized that there was no way I was going to debunk Jack's work.   But in the process of doing a lot of research on industrial hemp and medical marijuana and working with the Hemp Initiative, I had come across a lot of research and citations about entheogens. At one point Jack had invited me – I think it was 1993 or 1994 – to the "Gathering of the Minds" convention at Chapman University in Orange County and Dr. Dennis McKenna was there and Timothy Leary and Bruce Eisner and a lot of these guys. I met many of them and walked out of there realizing that my entire time in high school and college doing psychedelics was misspent and that I hadn't been taking them properly. I had had glimpses of the full-blown experience, but I hadn't ever had one, at that time. So I left the "Gathering of the Minds" convention that evening setting out to prove them wrong. I scored some mushrooms that evening and sat in silent darkness and ate seven grams and blew my mind.

MB – That's a lot of mushrooms.

JI – Yes. It was like I had never taken them before. To use the old cliché that Terence McKenna used to use, it was like all the other times I had done them before, it was like sitting out on the porch of the house of psychedelics but never having entered. But that night I entered and explored the house and the attic and the basement and the backyard and everything else. It was a pretty intense experience that really changed my course in life. I had done a lot of LSD and things like that in high school and early college and then at one point I stopped because I believed the propaganda out there that if you "take LSD seven times that you're legally insane" and all that garbage. So coming across all the research through Jack – Peter Stafford's *Psychedelic Encyclopedia* and Richard Even Schultes' *Plants of the Gods* were probably the first books that I read that had a lot of information on psychedelics. I started reading those and realized that there was just a massive amount of propaganda in the public arena. Out of personal interest, at that point, and having had the full-blown experience, I had started collecting books and doing a lot of research on the subject. I realized that while Allegro had some errors in his research, the majority of his work was correct.

In *Astrotheology & Shamanism* we show a lot of his correlations to be correct. Then in 2006 Michael Hoffman and I co-wrote an article "Wasson and Allegro on the Tree of Knowledge as Amanita" that showed that Wasson was incorrect on his attack on Allegro, and my new book, *The Holy Mushroom: Evidence of Mushrooms in Judeo-Christianity* follows that up and debunks all of the academic attacks on Allegro's entheogenic citations as well as all of the attacks by Gordon Wasson and Jonathan Ott and people like that. Jonathan Ott has always been one of my big heroes but unfortunately he still holds tight to the view that Allegro was a charlatan. So this book is really an opportunity, having worked with John Allegro's daughter for the last four years, to present his side of the story for the first time from what we found in our research.

MB – I definitely want to get into what John Allegro's research was and what some of the primary ideas are there. But before we get into that, I want to ask you, seeing as how you were doing all this research on early Christianity, personally, did you come from a religious or spiritual family? From what you said before, it sounds like your entryway into this was through your own personal experiences with entheogens that got you into this subject matter.

JI – Ironically, my parents were the kind of believers who believe just in case it's not bullshit – that type of thing.

MB – So they were using it as insurance.

JI – Yeah, exactly. But when I was a small child, I went to a Seventh Day Adventist school simply because it was the best school in the area. Everyday they had Bible study and you had to do prayer and you left at noon on Friday because Saturday was the Sabbath and you didn't do anything on Friday afternoon and you had to rest Friday evening. So I grew up indoctrinated completely in Christian beliefs and even later on when I wasn't a part of the Seventh Day Adventist's Christian school, I had gone to church for some time with my mom. But when I got into high school, I started having a lot of doubts. A lot of the things just didn't make sense. I remember the first time I heard the term "agnostic" and I thought, "Yeah! That makes a lot of sense."

At first I looked at Buddhist and Hindu philosophies and aligned toward them for a little while. With my experiences with psychedelics in high school, I had never heard that psychedelic drugs were used religiously. I had maybe heard of peyote, and even that was "just a drug" – we were just kids and we didn't know that it was associated with the Native Americans and hundreds of years of religious use. It was that path of experimentation and Christianity that combined when I came across Jack Herer's work. Jack told me that Jesus was never an historical character, and that he was an anthropomorphism of the male phallus and the mushroom.

At first, I thought this was ludicrous, and then later thought that perhaps both of them could be true: Jesus was both a real person and a symbol for these other ideas. Somewhere about 2002 or 2003 I was preparing the research for writing my book (*Astrotheology & Shamanism*, 2006, with Andrew Rutajit), and I'd been buried in books for many months analyzing the ancient stories and myths. Every time that I tried to literalize the histories of the characters I got more confused. This is not to say that none of the characters aren't real and some of the histories aren't real, because some of them are – but most of the characters in the Bible are not. When I stopped trying to literalize them and put this presumption on this document that we call the Bible, then suddenly I started perceiving things in a totally new perspective. I started going back over all of my notes and research and switching from analyzing the Bible from a literal/historical position to a mythological/fictitious position, just like we would with Zeus or Odin or Horus or any of the ancient gods.

That was really a turning point for me at that time because suddenly, instead of looking at all of the differences between the different religions and their mythology, I started to see their similarities. The similarities just started to stand out. Everything from the Bwiti in Africa who use iboga to Siberian shamans who use *Amanita muscaria* mushrooms to the Hindus and their *soma* and their *bhang* to the Native Americans with their peyote and the South Americans with their ayahuasca and San Pedro and dozens of other plants. I started to realize that many of them had their Eucharist and their "Tree of Life" or "Tree of Fire" or "Tree of Knowledge" story, such as the Yggdrasil tree and things like that. So there were these recurring themes throughout religion and these visionary experiences where a plant or a bush or tree would talk to them. Jesus was hung on a tree and was the son of a carpenter . . . all these different [sort of] things.

Eventually that led me into what is known as archeoastronomy and astrotheology. Archeoastronomy is ancient knowledge of the stars and the constellations, the measurement of time, the creation of calendars and things like that. Astrotheology is how the ancients anthropomorphized the stars and constellations and the sun and the moon and planets as gods. Today we have "Thor's Day" because Thursday was named after the god Thor. And Wednesday is "Woden's Day/Odin's Day," Friday is "Freya's Day," Saturday is "Saturn's Day," named after the planet/god Saturn. Then you start to look at when all these religions worship and it's interesting because the Jews worship on Saturday, which beckons back to the Roman times of Saturnalian worship, and then the Christians worship on Sunday, which used to be on the Sabbath or Saturday.   But Christianity is actually an anthropomorphism of the sun and Jesus has the same characteristics as the sun: He's born on the Winter Solstice, born under a virgin – Jesus is born from a virgin and the sun rises under the constellation Virgo on Christmas morning, about 6 am.   So there are all these correlations that I started to see and all the pieces began to come together in a way that I could just see what Allegro was attempting to do in his vision of creating a grand unified theory of religion.

MB – So then the more familiar you became with all these details from the other traditions and really understanding what the context was for the development of early Christianity, Allegro's ideas began to seem more plausible to you.

JI – Yes. For instance with the issue of the tree – Jesus is crucified on a tree as well as a cross – when we look in ancient times, besides the association with the carpenter, so many of the ancient myths were associated with tree worship. Odin, or Woden, was hung on a tree as well and speared. Then you have Shiva whose penis was severed in the forest and Astarte/Ashura whose name means sacred tree or sacred forest, Joseph Smith from the Mormons discovers his golden plates in the forest (in more modern times), and that's just a handful. We mention many more in the book that all relate to trees. Interestingly, all of the trees held sacred and associated with ancient mythology are also the host trees for *Amanita muscaria* and *Pantherina* mushrooms. The birch, the fir, the cedar, the pine and the oak are the primary trees worshiped in antiquity in all these different cultures and those are the trees that the mushrooms grow in symbiotic relationships with.

MB – So let's get back to your study of John Allegro's work on the Dead Sea Scrolls and what the significance of the scrolls is, along with John's interpretation and really how challenging that became for those who didn't want him to be publishing his information.

JI – The disinformation out there is that John Allegro was an Italian Jew who had it out against Christianity and all of this stuff. But actually his real background is that he was English and French. He grew up and had gone into the Royal Navy in World War II and was sort of a self-appointed boat chaplain, and when he got out of the navy he went to study for the Methodist ministry. While he was studying for the ministry, he was studying ancient Hebraic languages, and his studies made him start questioning his religious convictions. He eventually left the seminary and went to the University of Manchester to concentrate on ancient languages. There he won a first-class Honors Degree in Oriental Studies, and a Masters Degree for his work on the Balaam Oracles back in the early 1950's. After that he went to Oxford to begin his doctorate.

In 1947 the Dead Sea Scrolls were discovered and there was a big stir about them but no effort was made to create a really centralized effort to study and translate them until about 1953. I think it was Father Milik and Father de Vaux at the Vatican's Ecole Biblique who were attempting to set up a team of translators and they contacted Oxford. John's professor at Oxford recommended him as the British representative for the Dead Sea Scrolls team.

At that point he was already questioning his religious convictions, so by the time he got there, he was pretty much the only one who considered himself agnostic. All the rest, with the exception of maybe one or two Protestant scholars, were Catholic priests or had rankings within the Catholic Church. So Allegro took a different outlook from them from the beginning. In my humble opinion, I think Allegro was a lot more unbiased in his approach in looking at the Dead Sea Scrolls and he saw a lot of correlations that the others didn't want to see, such as the "teacher of righteousness" being hung on a tree in execution and the similarities between Joshua Bin Pandera and Joshua Bin Nun and the "Jesus" character. So that set him researching all these correlations between the Qumran sects and the Dead Sea Scrolls and Christianity and other religions.

So, in the late 1950's, he said on a radio show that this crucifixion of the "Teacher of Righteousness" in the Dead Sea Scrolls, along with many other similarities between the Gospel stories and the sectarian writings in the Scrolls, made it likely that Jesus' story was modeled on earlier traditions and practices in other words, the Christian story of Jesus's crucifixion was unoriginal. And like I said earlier, Odin/Woden was also crucified on a tree and speared in Norse mythology. But basically, he came out and said publicly that Christianity was partly based on existing messianic themes found in other, sometimes older, traditions. Because his work on the Scrolls gave him inside knowledge that hadn't all been published yet, and given that the other translators were nearly all Catholics (and all were Christians), they all turned and jumped on him in the press and basically lambasted him.

But Allegro fought them over the release of the scrolls and the right of scholars everywhere to discuss their interpretation from 1953 until his death in February, 1988, and never lived to see the scrolls released. For a long time, he was the only member of the Dead Sea Scrolls research team to publish anything on the scrolls. Allegro had published all of his translations by 1968 and started work on *The Sacred Mushroom and the Cross*. But from 1968 until the Huntington Library released the photographs of the Dead Sea Scrolls in 1991, nothing much had really gone public from the scrolls and the rest of the translating team held onto their translations until 1997. So it was a huge scandal that went on for nearly 50 years. Allegro was really the one who fought for decades for the public's access to the scrolls and other scholars' access to the scrolls, as well as just bringing attention to the scrolls in general. The suppression of the scrolls was so severe that, without Allegro's work, not many people would have ever known much about them.

MB – In the discovery of the Dead Sea Scrolls, the Catholic Church was looking for early Christian texts? What were they hoping to find?

JI - Well, the Catholic Church, as they have always been looking for up to and including the present day, was looking for proof of the historicity of the existence of Jesus Christ, this character. The Catholic Church, and Christianity in general, has been looking to prove the existence of Jesus for two millennia. The early Gnostics and many of the early religious groups in Judea and around Rome didn't believe that Jesus was a real person. In fact, John Lamb Lash has written a really excellent book that was published a couple years ago called *Not in His Image* that goes into the Gnostics and their use of entheogens and how their beliefs are actually much older than the Christians and are not derived from Christianity as many scholars wrongly assume. And that is precisely what John Allegro proposed with *The Dead Sea Scrolls and the Christian Myth* in 1979, if I remember correctly.

MB – And with John Lash's work, what did he say the Gnostics were making use of in their ceremonies?

JI – He argues that, if I recall correctly, it was *Amanita muscaria* and possibly psilocybin, but I don't recall directly as I wasn't focusing on his entheogen analysis – he might have gotten into ergot and the Eleusinian Mysteries, which Peter Webster has substantiated more recently with his work on ergot. But I think that ergot and amanita were the primary things he was discussing there.

MB – Getting back to John Allegro, he said that Jesus was not an historical person and the mythology surrounding him is really coded symbolism for the amanita mushroom and its use as a sacrament.

JI – That was his argument and I don't necessarily agree with his interpretation of the encoding. He believed that it was a small sect that created much of the Jesus myth and then enshrouded the mushroom in that story, but I think at the same time, which he does go into with the Gnostics and some of the other groups, I think that a lot of the mythology is derived from sun worship and the solstice and equinox celebrations. For example, I think that the cross itself is a symbol of the solstices and equinoxes. At any rate, Allegro argued that the character of Jesus certainly wasn't real and he mentioned several different things that he represented – sun worship, the phallus and the mushroom.

A lot of people started tearing Allegro apart because of his argument for the relationship of the Jesus character to fertility cults. Critics claimed that there really just wasn't any evidence for this fertility cult in ancient Judea, but the reality is that the Bible is filled with mention of this ancient cult of Ashera and Ba'al. These were shamanic goddess-worshiping cults that the Christians later demonized and called their followers devil worshipers and things like that. The whole history of Ashera and Astarte and Ba'al and Balpeor is really so badly misconstrued.

Eventually I started researching the fertility aspects of Allegro's research and found a history starting from the late 1780's and going all the way up to today of scholars who argued, like Allegro, that fertility cults played a role in the religion. Dr. Richard Paine Knight published his thesis in 1786, and he was attacked so severely for it that he personally went around and recalled all of his books that he had sold, and it didn't reappear until the late 1800's. There were other scholars: Hargrave Jennings and B.Z. Goldberg, and an excellent book by Thomas Inman, *Ancient Pagan and Christian Symbolism* goes deep into this stuff, and Clifford Howard – there are just so many excellent publications on this topic. For some reason, except for possibly Richard Paine Knight, Allegro seems to have taken the brunt of attacks for this proposal, even though there were at least a hundred books on the subject published over the last 230 years.

MB – When Allegro published, it sounds like people were more concerned about his association between Jesus and fertility cults than necessarily about the mushroom issue.

JI – I think they were. He was saying that Yahweh was an ancient fertility god and he got a lot of flack for that. I just finished reading a book this week by a guy named Alan Edwardes who published a book in 1967, three years before Allegro published his *The Sacred Mushroom and the Cross*, called *Erotica Judaica: A Sexual History of the Jews*, and in this book Edwardes argues that Yahweh was indeed an ancient phallic god and he cites several other scholars as well in ancient texts and things like that too. It certainly wasn't Allegro's idea. He didn't just make this stuff up and there were two centuries worth of other scholars who had written about it. Overall, I think the fertility aspects were the brunt of where Allegro received his attacks from, though. Then to top it off, from the entheogen camp, when Allegro published *The Sacred Mushroom and the Cross*, the "grandfather of ethnomycology," R. Gordon Wasson, launched his public attack against Allegro. This is really what my new book, *The Holy Mushroom*, goes into, this divide or this "schism" between Wasson and Allegro.

MB – This just seems to be such a curious person to be attacking Allegro, because of course, Wasson was really the person who introduced psilocybin mushrooms to the modern West, in some respects, in that he was going down to Mexico and working with Maria Sabina talking about Mazatec mushroom use, and he himself wrote about how with the ancient Rig Veda, the Hindu text, the divine Soma is the amanita mushroom. So he was working in this area. It seems odd that he would be so intent on attacking Allegro rather than supporting him and saying, "Well look – here's evidence of another mushroom cult!" It seems like it would be right up his alley.

JI- Well, you would think so. And as Jack Herer points out, of course Soma in the Rig Veda is not a literal historical character, and Allegro pointed out that Jesus is not a historical character and there are so many similarities in the stories. But part of the excuse was that while Wasson could see no influence of his own work on Allegro's work, he suggested that Allegro plagiarized his ideas. The fact is that Wasson was only a minimal source in Allegro's research and his primary sources were Robert Graves, a friend of Wasson's, and Prof. John Ramsbottom from the London Botanical Museum, and both of them published their theses on mushrooms and religion in the 1950's, long before Wasson published *Soma*. What's interesting is that Wasson and guys like Jonathan Ott have attacked Allegro for plagiarizing *Soma*, but what they don't realize, and what I've evidenced in my new book, is that Allegro first went public with his thesis in newspaper articles in 1967, before Wasson's *Soma* went to print. So it's a pretty incredible tale to tell that Allegro plagiarized all this stuff from Wasson. In fact, the Allegro archives in the Allegro estate show personal notes from John as beginning this research long before he went public in 1967.

There's been a great deal of disinformation around Allegro and his research and background on these things – like I mentioned earlier of people accusing him of being Jewish, so of course he's attacking Christianity. And another thing that I found was that Wasson had attacked Allegro for suggesting that, in Judeo-Christianity, the mushroom was related to the phallus. For so many years Wasson's book *Mushrooms, Russia and History* was just so far out of reach for people, but I was able to get a copy of that and start looking at Wasson's research. Much to my surprise, back in 1957, we see Wasson publishing 31 pages on cultures who worship mushrooms as a phallus, including Arabic cultures. So what Wasson did was draw this very fine line between Judeo-Christianity and the rest of his studies. This fine line in Wasson's mind was not crossable under any circumstances.

MB – So Wasson would defend that regardless of what evidence Allegro might present, then.

JI – On a deeper level, Wasson, in *Soma*, had proposed that the influence of the mushroom cult in Judeo-Christianity was limited to 1,000 B.C.E. and the Garden of Eden story. I checked all of Wasson's publications and could not find anywhere that he deviated from that position in 33 years. Wasson published *Soma* in 1968, and in 1970 Allegro published *The Sacred Mushroom and the Cross*. If Allegro is correct that mushroom use was present in Christianity, and not just limited to some ancient time period of the "Garden of Eden," then Wasson's own research in *Soma* must be incorrect – including his proposed limiting date of mushroom use to 1000 BCE.

So Wasson has a motive for attacking Allegro, and to further matters, it appears that Wasson was using the publication of Allegro's book to further advertise his own. In fact, in one of the letters that Wasson wrote to the *Times Literary Supplement*, there are four paragraphs where he's literally bragging about himself and his work and its extravagant publication. What he doesn't realize is that Allegro could have argued the same thing against him with the Dead Sea Scrolls and his own background and history of research. By that time, Allegro had already published probably seven or eight books, so Allegro was no amateur and was certainly an honored academic, in fact.

As we dug further in Wasson's research, Michael Hoffman and I found out that Wasson was the Vice President to J.P. Morgan Bank, which is today J.P. Morgan Chase, and in my opinion, one of the most corrupt banks in history. Wasson was one these money changers for this bank and close friends with J.P. Morgan. And on top of that, Wasson was also the account manager for the Vatican and worked directly with the Pope. So Wasson has these underlying connections that make his position seem very suspicious and it raises questions of why he might be so adamant about claiming mushroom use was not present in Christianity.

Wasson does some very suspicious things toward Allegro in his *Times Literary Supplement* as well. He attacks Allegro for citing Dr. Andrija Puharich, but in his attack, he calls Dr. Andrija Puharich "a man." He says, "Allegro cites *a man* on the history of amanita," and Dr. Puharich wrote the book, *The Sacred Mushroom: Key to the Door of Eternity*. What Wasson doesn't admit in this letter is that he worked with Puharich and was a personal friend and that Puharich wasn't just "a man" but was a medical doctor, and not only that, he was the captain of the US army chemical center at Edgewood Maryland collecting psychoactive substances for the M-K Ultra program! Wasson disparages Allegro while simultaneously protecting Puharich and using Puharich as a method to bash Allegro.

Another interesting little tid-bit that I found when I was researching all this was that for the last 30 years, one of the biggest propagators of all this disinformation and rumors has been Jonathan Ott. And like I said, I'm a big fan of Ott and am really disappointed about this aspect of his research. Jonathan Ott and Wasson perpetuated this rumor that Allegro made £20,000 – 30,000 from the publication of the serialization of *The Sacred Mushroom and the Cross* in what they called the *News of the World*, which is kind of like the American newspaper, *The Inquirer*. Well, first off, there was no publication in the *News of the World* of the serialization by Allegro. He published in *The Sunday Mirror*. It was published in four series. We checked the archives in the Allegro estate and there was no record of a £30,000 payment. And Wasson's allegations state that Allegro's headlines splashed the front pages each week with "Jesus Only a Penis!" None of Allegro's headlines made the front page, nor did they state the outrageous claims made by Wasson. So Wasson was really the one putting all of this information out there.

Now, to back up a step, before Allegro's article was even printed in *The Sunday Mirror*, Wasson was sending Allegro's so-called financial information to Helix Investments Ltd. in Canada, starting in February of 1970. So Wasson, for some reason – and I don't even care to research why – but for some reason, Wasson is sending what he thinks is Allegro's private financial information to an investment firm to investigate Allegro's background on how much he's making from the publication of the serialization. But ironically, as it turns out, *The Sunday Mirror* is of the same reputation as *Life* magazine of the famous May 1957 "Seeking the Magic Mushroom" article that Wasson himself launched his own career with. So there are all of these parallels where Wasson attacks Allegro for doing the exact same thing as him. Wasson made (*a minimum of*) $378,000 in today's money off of 412 copies of *Mushrooms, Russia and History* and then he attacked Allegro for profiteering from mushroom research!

MB – That sounds like a very bizarre and twisted tale, and this is all documented in your new book, The Holy Mushroom?

JI – It's all documented in *excruciating* detail. Everything is footnoted and cited as far as I could take it in every possible direction.

MB – It sounds like it's going to be a very important contribution to our understanding of the history of mycology and the relationships between entheogenic mushrooms and religion in the West.

Going back to the idea that Allegro was promoting that ultimately Jesus was not a real person, Jesus was an amanita mushroom (among other things that he is arguing in his body of work), I'm thinking about your film, The Pharmacratic Inquisition, *here – one of the things that strikes me about the film is the visual presentation of images that you have there of images from Christian frescos and artworks, and there seem to be images of amanita mushrooms pretty much all over the place. It presents this interesting question: Maybe they really are using amanita mushrooms within the Catholic Church. If Jesus really was a mushroom, were they really using it in the Catholic Chruch? What kind of evidence do we have for that? Did it last for some time? Do they still do it? Could we go to the Pope and say, "Hey, Pope, tell us about the amanita!" and what would the Pope say?*

JI – As far as mushroom use goes and documentation, the oldest instance of clear textual documentation that we have in the Judeo-Christian/Islamic tradition comes from a book called *The Mishkat* that Prof. John Rush talks about in his new book, *Failed God*. In this text Mohammed was asked, "What are mushrooms?" and he answers that mushrooms are a type of *manna* that allows man "to see."

Earlier this year Benny Shanon published his article, I think it was called "Entheogens and the Bible," that argued that Moses was using (in opposition to Allegro's view that Moses was not an historical figure) an ayahuasca analog made of Syrian rue and acacia. He presents evidence in his article that there is a rabbi from the 12th century who discussed *manna* and other religious persons at the time using drugs to achieve religious states of consciousness. So this is another textual piece of evidence.

And then the last instance that we have – so there are three documents total that we have to prove now – and none of these were available when Allegro published *The Sacred Mushroom and the Cross*, none of these were known about, at least, not to the entheogen community – and the newest one that we have was published in 1596 or 1597 by Ivan Vysensicyi from the Xiropotamou monastery on the Mt. Athos peninsula in Greece where he flat out discusses "the holy mushroom," and hence the name of my new book, *The Holy Mushroom*. It even talks about how he announced the holy mushroom to all of Christendom at the time. So here we have a document talking about the mushroom openly and in fact showing the Greek Orthodox Christians using the mushrooms to fight the materialistic Latins (Roman Catholics), as they call them in this document, as the Latins were money-driven and the Greeks were spiritual. This mushroom rises up out of the table and stops the Latin bishops from taking over the monastery. The end of this document talks about how the miracle of the holy mushroom was announced to all of Christianity and the multitudes were healed by the mere possibility of being able to taste the holy mushroom. So we do have documentation today of it, whereas we didn't before.

MB – Let's go back to the Catholic Church itself. Was the amanita used as a Eucharist in the Church? Is it possible that there are people in the Catholic Church today who would admit to this that, yes, this is a possibility.

JI – In *The Holy Mushroom* I'm publishing 43 images, about 37 of which have never been published before as far as entheogenic research, where I present mushroom trees and such things. I argue, with the presentation of the documentation that we have now, along with the history of mushroom use that we have from Russia to the British Isles, what we have was not a cult as Wasson and Allegro argued. It was not just fringe heretical sects. It was widespread.

One of the things that Wasson tried to use to argue that amanita was not in Christianity was over the Plaincourault fresco. What he said was that representations of Adam and Eve in the Garden of Eden are about the *Amanita muscaria* except for the Plaincourault fresco. The Plaincourault fresco was a 13th century fresco from Plaincourault, France that shows Adam and Eve on either side of a very distinct *Amanita muscaria* mushroom.

The Plaincourault Fresco, clearly showing *Amanita* mushrooms – image from Wasson's *Soma*

Between Wasson and Erwin Panofsky, they created this ridiculous diatribe about how mycologists don't study art, so therefore they couldn't possibly know that this is just a copy of earlier artwork and it's just fortuitous that they painted this amanita and there's no chance that they could have really known about it, which is all based on assumption. They didn't do any kind of study to back this assumption. So Wasson and Panofsky went off saying that there was no way this could represent an amanita mushroom.

Amanita muscaria, fresh.

Well, Allegro disagreed and found a letter that Wasson had written to Prof. John Ramsbottom at the London Botanical Museum stating that, "Rightly or wrongly, we're going to dismiss the fresco." So, Allegro saw Wasson's letter, and finds Wasson waffling over the entire position, and that is what made Wasson really go berserk over the entire issues (which is kind of funny as the word *berserk* comes form berserkers which is also related to amanita use and is also something that Wasson argued against). There are all of these subtle ties that bring everything together throughout the research. Anyway, through texts, we can bring amanita use up to the 16th century, and through art, up to the 1800's.

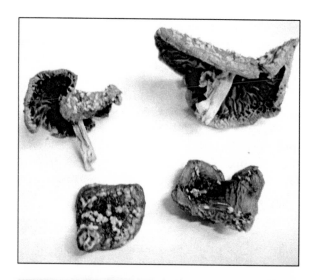

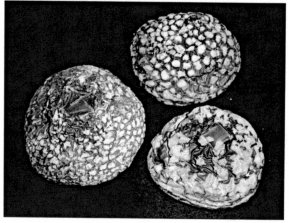

Dried *amanitas.*

MB – And that's something that's really striking in your film – how prevalent images of amanita mushrooms appear to be in artwork from European religious history associated with Christianity.

JI – Well wait until you read John Rush's book, *Failed God*. He's 100% behind Allegro. In fact, he's the first academic to go 100% in support of Allegro's mushroom thesis and he argues that Jesus was in fact a mushroom.

Dr. Rush is conducting a study of churches throughout the U.S. and he argues that you can find the mushroom symbolism even in churches built today. He's working on another project to present that research.

Getting back to the Plaincourault fresco and tying it back to the Catholic Church, the Chapel of Plaincourault was built by the Knights of Malta, who are headquartered in Vatican City to the present day. So against what scholars have argued that if the mushroom was used at all in Christianity, it was only with fringe heretical sects, but if the Plaincourault fresco was made by the Knights of Malta and we deny Wasson and Panofsky's argument that it isn't an amanita mushroom, which it obviously is, we have a direct tie to the Vatican through the Knights of Malta up to the 13th century. And then we begin to see a pattern, in my opinion, of why it was important to Wasson to try and disprove Allegro.

MB - The question to me is: What happened? If Jesus was an amanita mushroom and if people were using the amanita and this was their sacrament and this knowledge and experience was shared, what happened? Because as we all know, Christian sects don't look too kindly on the sacramental ingestion of entheogens at this point in time, and certainly there seems to be a whole history of the "pharmacratic inquisition" of Christian forces really coming down hard on pagans, shamans, witchcraft, etc. and saying that this is the Devil's work. How did we get from A to B here?

JI – Well it's kind of like how you see on the news when you see a Republican getting busted for being a pedophile or some sex scandal and they are the ones out there preaching the loudest about how evil these things are. They put up the most talk, but they're getting busted for exactly that. He who is making the most noise is probably the most suspicious.

As far as how we got into this situation, if we look at the ancient mystery schools and how they shrouded everything in secrecy, and rising up out of ancient shamanism, I think the secrecy – well, this is where I tie it in to Dr. James DeMeo's book, *Saharasia* and his research. What he shows is that around 4,000 B.C.E. it's the start of the desertification of the Saharasian, or Saharan and Asian, desert region, and this created environmental tension that stirred people from matrist cultures to warring patrist cultures. And then you have the segregation of males and females, the suppression of sex, the rise of patriarchal religions and secret societies and things like that.

So that's really the point that we argued in the first book, *Astrotheology and Shamanism*. This is what really ties this shift. As long as there's this overlying paternal father and god figure, there is always going to be the jealous god, the warring god, suppressing the female. This is what's enshrouded around the Catholic Church. So what I'm getting at is that we can hypothesize that in the inner levels of the Catholic Church, we have initiates into the ancient mystery schools and therefore they would have a lot of knowledge about these mushrooms.

And I want to make it clear that we don't just argue for amanita mushrooms. We argue the use of many entheogens, including psilocybe mushrooms. I think that very clearly the *manna* that was found in the wilderness was psilocybe mushrooms: cubensis mushrooms. When we look at that passage in the Bible (Deut 8:16) and see what word that was used for wilderness or desert, it's a Hebrew word, "midbar," which translates into cow pasture, and that's something that anyone can look up in *Strong's Concordance* and can verify (*Strong's* H4057). There are very strong correlations to other substances as well. Many of the art depictions from France very strongly suggest both amanita and psilocybin/psilocybe use. We really feel that it was a combination of use of amanita and psilocybe use if not possibly other substances such as Syrian Rue and opium as well.

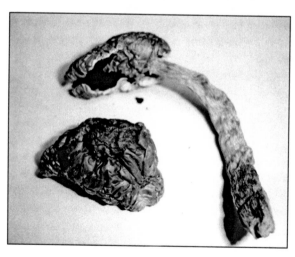

Dried *psilocybe* mushrooms

And we have in the book of Genesis (30:14-17) the story of the mandrake with Rachel and Leah. They're arguing over who's going to have sex with Leah's husband, so Leah buys a night with her own husband with some mandrake. Mandrakes are not only psychoactive psychedelically speaking, but they're also an aphrodisiac. So it's a very interesting story of these two women arguing over who was going to have sex with this man, I think it was Jacob, and the use of these mandrakes in the Book of Genesis. Certainly there's use of these things in the fertility cults.

MB – Bringing it up to where we are today, what do you think this means for us here and now, both in terms of our understanding of religion or our understanding of spiritual experience, and our understanding of our idea of freedom? How would you tie this in to where we are at?

JI – I think it has everything to do with what you just said with regard to religion and spirituality and freedom. My personal feeling is that the enteogenic experience *is* the religious experience. And having knowledge of what the Eucharist really is and what *manna* really is, instead of taking the placebo cracker and wine, I think it brings a whole new level of meaning and a return to the ancient understandings of religion as a whole and how we can each have our own individual connection with whatever it is, the Spirit or Gaia, or whatever this connection is. In that, this truth is going to give us freedom because the religious dogmas are no longer going to be able to enslave us mentally.

When people start to realize that Christianity and all of these ancient religions, paganism, fertility cults, sun worship, all of them are based on similar ideas, then we can get back to the core of what these religions are all about – self-discovery and bettering yourself as a human being and not killing your next door neighbor because he worships a different god than you, or calls the same god a different name. It can have a huge impact as far as human understanding of religion and freedom of consciousness. Ironically, one of the psilocybe mushrooms is the "liberty cap" and it is associated with the Phrygian cap, which is a symbol of freedom.

MB – So I guess you would say in putting out these ideas about Christianity, you're really trying to correct some of our interpretations of Christianity and present alternative possibilities of what it might all really be. And in getting this information out into the public, we're not only increasing our knowledge of Christianity, but also providing an argument for why entheogens should be respected as spiritual catalysts as it's actually part of our history and of our traditions that we've grown up in and around.

JI – Yes, exactly. And now with the evidence of the holy mushroom in Christianity, we can finally argue that Christianity is no exception, and even the "established churches" will have to start accepting the holy mushroom as part of Christian worship. And we're going to have to look at entirely new methods, which I think you know all too well, of proposing an approach to how we all look at religion and how we practice our own spirituality.

MB – If we could talk personally for a minute here, how would you say your own life has been impacted spiritually through entheogens?

JI – Well, you know, we all grow up with issues that, being human, require us to work through them to better ourselves and grow and learn about ourselves. As far as my personal growth and learning of my strengths and weaknesses and my faults and positives as well, it's been key in learning to accept myself for who I am as well as learning things about the universe and life in general that I would have never seen without these substances, in my opinion. I don't really think that there's any one substance. All of the different entheogens create their own experiences and take you into their own worlds, so within that, every new entheogen takes you into new worlds and new things to learn.

MB – Have you attempted, in any way, to reconcile this in any way with your religious upbringing as a child?

JI – Oh yeah . . . a long time ago. Basically, I've taken up my own path. I like to study a lot of ancient religions. I'm more along the lines of gnostic with a lower case g, not a capital dogmatic Gnostic. Gnostic comes from the word *gnosis*, from which we get the word knowledge. It's the act of learning and constantly striving to know what's out there. To me, the real religion is learning how much you don't know and how much there is to learn and always striving to learn more. You can spend your entire lifetime learning this one field without realizing there are all these other fields out there. So why not do something that is useful to everyone, and that's expand our knowledge and education instead of striving for some jealous god from the Neolithic age who is sexually repressed and wants to kill us because we don't like his attitude.

MB – What do you see as the contribution you are making to this with your work with Gnostic Media?

JI – Oh, that's a loaded question! Hopefully it's making some change. Hopefully people find some benefit in my work and find some use and interest in it. As far as my so-called prediction on how it's going to impact society and religion and all of that, hopefully I'm not narcissistic enough, through my own entheogen use, to make a bloated claim, so I'll leave it at that.

MYCELIUM MESSIAH AND THE JESUS EXPERIENCE

An entheologue with

Dr. John A. Rush, Ph.D., N.D.

John A. Rush, Ph.D., N.D., is a Professor of Anthropology at Sierra College, Rocklin, California, teaching Physical Anthropology and Magic, Witchcraft and Religion. Dr. Rush's publications include *Clinical Anthropology: An Application of Anthropological Concepts within Clinical Settings* (1996), *Stress and Emotional Health: Applications of Clinical Anthropology* (1999), *Spiritual Tattoo: A Cultural History of Tattooing, Piercing, Scarification, Branding, and Implants* (2005), *The Twelve Gates: A Spiritual Passage through the Egyptian Books of the Dead* (2007), and *Failed God: Fractured Myth in a Fragile World* (2008). He is also a Naturopathic Doctor and Medical Hypnotherapist in private practice. His latest book, *Failed God*, explores the theory that Judeo-Christian-Islamic traditions are based on ritual use of entheogens. The original photographs in this interview were provided by Dr. Rush from his personal collection.

Martin Ball – Greetings, John, and welcome. Maybe you could get us started by telling us how you got into this field of research concerning entheogen use in Western traditions.

John Rush – This has been a long adventure for me. It began in the late 60's, and I actually didn't quite understand what was going on at that point in my academic career. But when I was in graduate school there was a priest who also had a degree in anthropology and he and I spent some time together. He said a lot of things that I didn't quite understand; many were veiled ideas, allusion, and so on. But then in 1970, John Allegro came out with his book, *The Sacred Mushroom and the Cross*, and it started to make more sense what this priest had been trying to tell me. I still didn't quite understand it and what it really meant. I just didn't know what to do with the information because I didn't have the necessary knowledge base.

MB – Could you recap what John Allegro's arguments were?

JR – As he was going through the Dead Sea Scrolls he was assigned to interpret, he came across references to substances and their connection to Jesus. There are references going back at least to the writings of the Essenes from 200 BCE right up to about 130 CE – somewhere in there. After reviewing these materials, Allegro made the argument that Jesus probably was not an historical person but a symbol for entheogenic experience, among other things.

I put all that aside and went on my merry way collecting information and reading the literature – particularly about other cultures using these substances. And then it became very strange in the sense that, OK, you have all these people using plants and fungi, we have this idea of shamanism, and of course many of these shamans are using these substances, and these shamans morph into priests when we get into Mesopotamia and so on. I can't imagine that they would have given up these substances and the "real" god showed up to talk to people. So these substances must have been used all along. It doesn't make sense that these sources of direct spiritual experience would suddenly drop out of use.

But I didn't really know how to put this out to the public. You have to be politically correct, I suppose. You don't want to lose your teaching position like what happened to Allegro. So I just put it aside and started to collect things, pictures and opinions. No reasonable person can ever think that the storyline connected to Jesus is factual history, so there had to be meaning in back of all this and that is where the icon, the art comes in.

In 2001 the picture started to become clearer for me. My wife and I went to Europe, and our purpose was to explore as many of the cathedrals and basilicas as we possibly could. This was exhaustive and at times clandestine research. One of the first cathedrals we went into in Rome was St. Maria Maggiore, and when we were looking at the mosaics, something jumped out at me. This particular scene in that cathedral, as I recall it, showed a picture of Abraham and his wife, and he's next to a table. This is the story of Abraham going off and ending up in Sodom and all these angels come in and he's negotiating with God over who's going to get destroyed and so on. At any rate, I took a close look at this particular mosaic and noticed on the table were what looked like three triangular loaves of bread; Jesus usually has round loaves. But when you look closely at them, they've got stems. They're mushrooms!

So, we took some pictures here, catacombs, St. Pete's, etc., left Rome and went up the coast to Ravenna. In Ravenna is St. Apollinaire, and in the main hall within the church (Apse), there is a mosaic that shows an inverted mushroom; there is no doubt it is a mushroom. Underneath that is the hand of God.

Detail of center top of previous image. Notice the inverted mushroom above the hand of God.

This motif, in more recent times—St. Apollinaire dates to about 550 CE—shows a cloud and hand of God. This motif was borrowed from ancient Egypt, and the heretic pharaoh Akhenaten and his sun disk, with rays, that terminate in hands holding an ankh, the Holy Mushroom, to his face and genitals.

Flanking the Hand of God at St. Apollinaire are Moses and Elijah, and if you look closely at their stoles, there's a mushroom image. In the stole of Elijah the mushroom is accompanied with the symbol "I" for Jesus. As you come down the mosaic you see Apollinarius as the saint and he's flanked by rocks that look like mushrooms. Now, I couldn't see this from the Nave. I couldn't see this until I got home in California, blew up the picture, and looked at it.

So many of these images are in these cathedrals and basilicas and people go by them every day. But they don't pay attention to them because they can't get close enough to see them. You can't bring a ladder into the church and examine them close up and personal. So these became what I call "visible invisible motifs." They're there, but you have to know what to look for, and you have to be able to get close enough to be able to see them. The same thing would occur with the *Book of Hours* and all these beautiful illustrated manuscripts. Very few people would have seen these things. So you can have lots of images that you don't have to explain to anybody because of limited access. Well, things have changed.

At any rate, the next place we entered was St. Mark's in Venice. When I walked into St. Mark's it was like walking into a psychedelic palace. I couldn't believe it. It's a functioning church and it's also a tourist attraction. You line up at the front door and they lead you through like sheep – you know, that's the way the system works.

My wife and I stopped at this one arch and we started looking up. It was up on the arch, and I turned to my wife and said, "Are you seeing what I'm seeing?" And she whispered, "Is that Jesus with a mushroom in his hand?" And I'm saying, "Yeah, you're seeing the same thing!" Now, my wife was skeptical about this, but not any more, not after seeing all these images; I now have 1600 images spanning 1,700 years, from 300 CE to 2000 CE.

No sooner were we able to clarify what we were witnessing when a woman came scooting out from the side saying, "Move along, move along." My wife responded, "What's the matter with you?" She says, "My duty is to get you to move along from here."

So we move along. We were there just before the afternoon siesta. In Europe they always take a couple hours off in the afternoon, close the shops, and take a nap or break. We took advantage of that, going back into the church and I got some pictures.

Now, during our first trip to the church, as you walk into St. Mark's, there are, to the right, up in the domes, the scenes of the creation, but they were roped off. So I'm leaning over the rope, trying to look up at the dome, and this little old lady asks, "Oh, do you want to see?" I say, "Yeah!" She took down the rope and I came in and said, "Can I take a picture?" She turned around and walked away, so I got a picture.

Now, in this picture, high up in the ceiling, you can see Adam and Eve, the creation story. This is in the sequel to the *Failed God* book, which will come out in about a year called *The Mushroom in Christian Art*, where I look at numerous – I think there are now about 213 pictures, stained glass images, and so on with mushrooms. In this particular image in that dome, Eve is pointing at the snake and she's pointing at Adam. Adam then is pointing at the Tree of Life. And what is it? It's a mushroom! And there it was, right there in front, but safe, too far for anyone to examine. This is the visible/invisible motif.

We went to numerous cathedrals throughout Europe and took lots of pictures, and when back in California, I was shocked. I just didn't know what to do with the information. How do you present this to the world? Because the consequences of this, as I mention in the preface to the *Failed God*, is if the historians would get off the dime here and stop being politically correct, and mention this information, we could come to an entirely new understanding of Western religion and Western Civilization in general.

I'm also getting the impression that many of these scholars, whether they're at Harvard or elsewhere, as they're going through graduate school, they don't want to upset their thesis advisors. So they simply go along with the interpretations they've been given. They're not thinking about these things. They're not really looking at them. I have emailed many historians at universities in the US. I asked if there was awareness of this motif, the mushroom in Christian art. No one admits to being aware of this.

MB – So you've found something that is, apparently, everywhere. You've found these images all throughout Europe, you've collected them, but nobody's actually studied this and looked at this and said, "What are all these mushrooms doing in Christian art?"

JR – Right! I had thought that other people, Carl Ruck and so forth, had explored the Christian art in detail, or some art historian had done this. There have been pictures scattered here and there and certainly more recent materials, like Jan Irvin's, *The Holy Mushroom*. But unlike other aspects of icons, for example, colors, facial features, shapes of mountains, position of hands, and so on, no texts, that I'm aware off, currently used in undergraduate or graduate courses mention the mushroom, although everything else is held up to close scrutiny. In *Apples of Apollo* and *Hidden World* they certainly mention Old and New Testament connections to Christianity. These works, and others, certainly lay a foundation for understanding the origins, depth, and shamanic purposes connected to folk tales which then help us understand early rituals in the Christian tradition.

Another issue is how the mushroom is presented. See, they present their material in a very academic way, and I'm not criticizing this, but it is preaching to the choir, which is great in the academic world. Don't get me wrong. These researchers—Ruck, Staples, Irvin, Heinrich, yourself, and many others have done ground breaking work showing that Christianity is a composite of earlier systems complete with entheogens. I wrote *Failed God* in a way to get people's attention. I went out of my way to insult a few institutions, people, and so on, and if any one of them jumps at it, then we can open the mushroom up to public inspection. The only way we can get a public forum is to get media attention.

One of the things that is very, very important is this whole idea that the use of substances brought people to action and helped to establish the Catholic Church; we disagree on the details, but I think that most serious scholars would have to agree with the general premise. The Church branches through time, but still, the basis of it was the use of these substances. And it's not just *Amanita muscaria*. I think that amanita is used as a generic image that represents all the rest of the entheogens, whether it is cannabis, psilocybin, mandrake, or whatever it might be. I think it's a generic image. But within that you can see the psilocybin and so on. In that image with Jesus we encountered at St. Mark's basilica we saw, surrounding Jesus, psilocybin-type mushrooms.

Now, in the *Failed God* book, I didn't comment in great detail as to who some of the characters were in the images on the cover of the book and inside. The reason I didn't do this is because the book was getting too long. So I've gone back in *The Mushroom in Christian Art* and clarified some of these people and their symbolic values once entheogenic substances are computed into the formula.

For example, if you look at the cover of the book we can see Jesus with a woman and a man and various mushrooms.

Image from the cover of *Failed God*, by John Rush

The woman to the left is Eve and the gentleman to his right is Adam. You can see that Eve is looking at the mushroom between Jesus' feet and she's pointing at Jesus. Here we see Jesus holding a mushroom cap in his left hand and with his index finger pointing to the hole in his right hand, and his right index finger is pointing to himself. Now, pointing in Christian art is extremely important because it tells the viewer what to look at and what's important in the image. Right here, we have the statement, in the visual arts, saying that Jesus is the mushroom thus confirming Allegro's original contention.

Over the past few years, since 2001, when I collected these original images, I really had a debate within myself as to what to do with this. If this does get into the mainstream, what happens to Judaism, Christianity, Islam, once it becomes generally known that the basis for these traditions was mind-altering substances?

MB – It's radical. It's revolutionary.

JR – Yes it is! And this idea has been around for a long time. It's been around at least since Allegro, and there have been a number of books more forceful in presentation, but they've been ignored. I'm not sure if anybody can continue to ignore this. I know that the Archdiocese in Los Angeles has a copy of my book. I know they have a copy because I sent them one! And I sent a few copies out to some other people too – some art historians at rather prestigious universities—for them to take a look at this as well.

I guess I'm here to cause some trouble. We expect the scholars to get it right. And if they don't get it right the first time, reexamine your material and then get it right the second time, or however many times it takes. But they're not getting this right. You can still pick up modern textbooks and history books written within this past year and they present Mohammed as a real person, they present Jesus as a real person, and there just isn't any evidence. It makes much more sense to say they're symbols and characters.

Speaking of Mohammed, I'd been searching for years, and I found an image, painted in about 1325, of Mohammed standing on *Amanita muscaria* mushrooms. This is from Rashid al-Din's, *Jami al-Tawarikh* (Universal History). Now, in Islam, images are forbidden, and we can see why! And I have one *hadith* that refers to mushrooms. One translation says that it's an eye-wash, or whatever, but the problem is that the word "manna" is connected to it; I don't think any herbal remedy, an eye wash for example, qualifies as manna. I haven't seen it connected to anything that isn't mind-altering, sent down by the gods, or the Holy Ghost, or this type of thing.

The issue here, then, is, once the general populace gets the message, what happens to these traditions? As Schopenhauer said, "What is it that happens when you take someone's religion away from them?" Well, I have a cure for that. See, you don't have to give up the tradition. You just have to give it up as historical fact.

There are several levels to Christian art and there's a big story as to why the art exists in the first place. Early on you had the Iconoclasts who didn't want this art out there, going along with the second commandment in the Bible – the feeling that people would make these into idols and worship them. And this is what happened. There were images of saints and they were worshipped.

And then you run into the argument that shows up in 325 CE as to whether Jesus was a real person or all spirit or whatever. But really what this amounts to is the recognition that numerous groups had different experiences with the deity. There were many groups that, using these substances, couldn't really define what Jesus was. They certainly didn't have a picture of him. This idea of creating an image was distasteful for many simply because they're having an *experience*. Jesus was an experience. He wasn't a real person.

But in order to have a system you have to get people on the same page. This is where Constantine comes in. The Church would like us to believe that Constantine was a true believer and supporter of the Christian cause, but that is unlikely. The Catholic Church has always had contempt for the truth. I'm sure Constantine threatened Eusebius of Caesarea with death unless he brought this system together, to stop the fighting, which was a distraction from running his kingdom. So Eusebius and his crew went around locating books and trying to find the real Jesus, but they couldn't. This leads to book burning and forgeries. What I think they had to do was make this real; they had to make Jesus real. They had to put a face to him and create a standard.

There are no faces of Jesus in art until around 500 C.E. There apparently are some images before that, but they are of the saints. You see, the saint would take the substance and commune with God or Jesus. It wasn't Jesus who originally transfigured, as shown in the famous painting of Raphael (*Transfiguration* 1520 CE); it was the saints as amply displayed at St. Apollinaire and in other early works. Jesus wasn't there; he was an experience. And when he is given a face, the saints take second place. Jesus goes from a personal experience to historical fact by consensus vote after 325 CE and the council of Nicaea.

But let's get back to the different levels in the images, of which there are several. The first level has to do with what I call the exoteric rituals. These were for the average person. This is where you are supposed to believe in or have faith that the storyline is historical fact. That's what the Church wants you to think and the way they want you to interpret these images. However, if that's all there was to these images, then the average person would know what the priests know because everybody would know the rituals.

So there has to be another level in these pictures, and there is. It's the esoteric level. It's the level that the priests go through during ordination as they are introduced to these images and the deeper meaning of this tradition. Now I don't know exactly how they did this within these cathedrals or basilicas, but these were centers of initiation and so on. At St. Mark's there are special rooms on the second floor, with mosaics, roped off, and dark. These images were for educational purposes with the goal of finding God. So we've got the exoteric level and an esoteric level.

But there is another level, one more speculative. I believe there is a level dealing with botany, that is, locating and processing the mushroom and other substances. The basis of the original Christian worship was the mushroom and modern Catholic rituals are a reflection of this. As an example, in the 12th and 13th centuries there are a number of images of baby Jesus nursing from the Virgin Mary. When you look at these icons – and the scholars will tell you this too – you cannot look at these images and take them at face value; they are not pictures. When you see a tree, it isn't a tree. When you see Mary in these icons, it's not Mary. When you see Jesus, it's not Jesus. *It's what stands in back of these images.* And so, with Mary nursing Jesus, she represents the roots of the pine tree. So, you have St. Ann, Mary's mother, who is a pine tree, a Lebanese cedar tree, and the Lebanese cedar tree is connected to the god in the Old Testament. So you've got the Lebanese cedar tree's roots, which would be Mary, and Jesus who is synergistic off the roots – a mushroom growing from the roots of the tree. Now, the origin of this is actually Isis and Horus coming out of the Egyptian tradition where they were doing the same thing with their iconography.

I have another book called *The Twelve Gates* where I outline the Osiris round, which has to do with his murder by his brother Seth and what happens to him and so on, and in that work I redo the story a bit, that is, more clearly describe who or what Osiris is. Osiris is actually the mushroom incased in the roots of the Lebanese cedar tree when his casket is pitched up on the shore in Lebanon, so this is an important theme in Egyptian tradition. The whole idea of Isis and Horus is similar to Mary and Jesus. Isis is the throne upon which the Pharaoh sits. Mother Mary is the throne upon which Jesus sits. So you can see the similarity here of the roots and the fruits that come from this. It's a mushroom and its symbiotic host tree.

So we have these various levels, if you will, in the art. Now, in the *Mushroom in Christian Art* book, which will be out in about a year, I have a chapter where the individual can actually go through these images in sequence, identify with these images, and have a spiritual experience. When you give up the Christian storyline as history, and you look at what lies behind these images, a spiritual experience awaits.

MB – A question that comes to mind immediately with all of this is: How did we get so confused as to what this actual tradition is? And by a point of comparison, let's go over to India and take the case of Shiva. Here we have a mythological figure, obviously a god, and it's pretty clear when you look at the mythology and the iconography surrounding Shiva that he really does represent psychoactive plants and medicines. His followers, to this day, will use marijuana, or ganja, and bhang (ganja mixed with datura), and they'll use psilocybin mushrooms. They're seeking altered states of consciousness using meditation and there's no confusion. Nobody says that Shiva is an historical figure. That's not an issue and they're still practicing these traditions today. So what happened in Christianity where we moved from actually ingesting psychoactive sacraments to getting this historical figure of Jesus and all of this that the Bible is literally true and we've got to take every word literally? We're completely ignorant about these images of Jesus and the mushrooms and nobody knows anything about it. How did we get so far from that original tradition? What happened?

JR – That's a wonderful question. We could start off by talking about Buddhism. If you were to ask a Buddhist monk if all the stories about Buddha were true, he would turn around and walk away from you. It's not the point that the story is true; it's what the story is trying to tell you that's is important.

Now, we get the exact opposite in the Christian tradition and the history behind it has been covered up. It seems to have come about like this: My belief is that someone, or maybe a small group of people, did defect from the Essenes. There may have been someone called John the Baptist. I mean, there *is* somebody who is connected to political things that went on with Herod's troops getting badly beat up and so on. Herod, fearing he might be challenged politically by the Baptist and his small group, had John murdered. John the Baptist was mentioned in connection with this event. After his death, the group fractured, leading to numerous groups based on the worship of the mushroom. This event, this original cult started sometime between 10 BCE and 32 BCE, and in a few years there would be numerous branches stemming from this.

MB – Maybe you could explain briefly who the Essenes were and their relationship to this?

JR – To understand the Essenes we have to go back to about 200 BCE. They were defectors from the Maccabees and they took a lot of written material out of the temple, and some of the writings were altered—so much for the divine word of God. And not only did they live in those caves in the Dead Sea, but they were in public as well. These people thought the world was coming to an end. "The world is coming to an end!" "Clean up your life!" and so on.

Now, in terms of the overall history of this group, there are better scholars to ask than me with respect to this. My interest is in the defectors. Who defected? I'm sure somebody did. It would have been sometime between the beginning of the current era, maybe 10 BCE to 32 CE. It may have been someone like John the Baptist or a small group. But whoever this person was, he was a priest. He goes into the wilderness, he's using these substances, obviously – they're mentioned throughout the Dead Sea Scrolls – and he comes to a very important conclusion and that is: If you eliminate all of the rules and regulations within Judaism or any of these systems, and you get rid of everything that separates people, what you're left with brings them together. I think this was a revelation that came to somebody, who then came out of the desert or wherever he came from, defected, and started to sell this idea. But he did it in a different way than you would expect. He is not running around and saying "Thou shalt not . . ." All the "shalt nots" divided people. What he did, instead, was pretty much what a Buddhist monk does and again, we've got the Silk Road and there are people traveling back and forth and someone like John the Baptist could have easily gone to India and obtained this information, or by just hanging around people in Basara or that area and picking up on a lot of this information.

But at any rate, he's not saying "Thou shalt not . . ." He's telling people stories and he's not saying anything to anyone unless they ask him a question. If they ask him "Should my brother share his wealth with me?" then he can talk. That's what a Buddhist monk does. Now, if you read the Gospels, and in particular if you read the Gnostic Gospel of Thomas, there's no history of Jesus in that Gospel. It's just him sitting there, and if someone asks him a question, then he tells a story. What a gentle way to get people thinking. Getting them to think and question. So he's getting them to think and he's telling them, "Forget about what you eat, forget about what you wear, you don't need a priest or a church, just be a decent human being, and when things come to an end, you'll be judged worthy." That's all he had to say. This simple message was perverted by the Church. God, in the three Western Traditions, Judaism, Christianity, and Islam comes first, and human decency comes second. In this sense, the deities connected to these traditions are demons.

MB – It's almost an anti-religion, in a sense. He's getting them to turn away from all these rules and regulations and "let's just focus on who you are."

JR – Actually, what the Baptist was promoting was the "old time religion," where the individual identifies with God, communicates with God, or perhaps becomes God. It's kind of like modern day encounter groups that the Baptist was probably running, rituals involving mind-altering substances. Now, in order for this system to sustain itself, he had to train people, because he's not going to be around forever. So he's running around for a few years, and he attracted maybe 100 people. It's unlikely that he would have attracted much more than this for the reason that he would have been unable to deal with them. You can only deal with so many people at any one time, and when you go above a certain number of people – and this is something that the historians miss –you can only deal with so many people at any one time because your brain can only process so much information. Group size is important here, because when it gets past, say, 100 people, then the leader can't keep in touch with everybody on a day-to-day basis. This is why early Christianity was not one group that simply got bigger and bigger; group dynamics do no support this position. I go into this in great detail in *The Mushroom in Christian Art*.

So, this leader, whoever he was, probably trained a number of people. Of course, in the Bible you get this number of 12 apostles, but that's probably astronomical and related to the zodiac. He had a couple people who had been thoroughly trained and the others had not. So, John the Baptist dies, and what happens to this group? It fractures. It fissions. And you have some of the people who had been trained taking some of the people with them to establish another group, maybe this was the Gnostics, maybe the Jesus or Christ cults—who knows. Then you have other people with lesser-trained individuals going in another direction.

Now it's these lesser-trained people who were getting into trouble. They did not have rites and rituals that were organized so you have a beginning, middle, and end to the rituals. They're probably using substances and you have people writhing on the ground after taking some of these substances, releasing demons and what not. And the pagans are seeing this and thinking that these people are quite weird, and not only that, they're worshiping a mushroom! Can you imagine the Greeks worshiping a grape? They didn't do that. They didn't think that any god lived in a grape. So, some of the behaviors of these early splinter groups, and I'm guessing at this, particularly those who ended up in groups with untrained leaders, probably caused a lot of trouble. And in their zealousness to teach people or whatever, they're probably going into shrines and busting up idols and whatnot and they're causing a lot of trouble. These are the ones persecuted.

So time goes on, and I'd say within probably 100 years or so you'd probably have 50 – 60 different groups doing slightly different things, an adaptive radiation you might say. The size would increase in individual groups and then they would fracture and fracture again. Some groups became extinct. Others became other traditions and changed. Some of the groups, even to this day, are worshiping John the Baptist and other things. You have, then, a number of groups out there and some survived and some didn't.

Now, it's like arguing politics – it's like arguing about McCain and Obama. You've got all these groups and they're arguing with one another because they're into the politics of truth. What's truth? What is Jesus all about? Who is he? What is he? And so on. You've got these arguments going back and forth and they get pretty heated. People get killed. Shrines get burnt down. It's difficult for a rational person to understand this behavior, but if you have your emotional eggs in one basket and someone is ripping it apart with their truth, well you get the point.

And then we get to the point where we have Constantine. Constantine was a thug who recruited a number of groups, who became the Catholics, to do his bidding. I don't believe he ever became a Christian and it is difficult to accept as truth any history generated within the Church for public consumption.

MB – What year was he?

JR – 312 CE up to about 336 CE – somewhere in there.
     He's got problems. He's trying to defend his kingdom. You've got these different groups pushing in, Goths, Vandals, and so on. Then to turn around and have to put out all these damn fires from the Christian groups and the Pagan groups fighting each other! He finally called a bunch of these people and said, "Look. You settle this, or I will settle it for you." And so what happened is that we have a number of groups who could probably argue about how many angels could sit on the head of a pin without killing each other and Eusebius was probably part of this. He was thrown in jail, threatened, probably with death, if he didn't cooperate, and so Eusebius helped to organize a number of these groups.
     To do this he had to go around and confiscate literature that contained the rites and rituals. He had to get everybody on the same page. You have groups that are thinking that Jesus was simply an essence, an experience, and not a real person. Then you've got this other group over here thinking that Jesus was a real person. By now we are, after all, a couple hundred years away from the alleged event – you can see how these people would be in intense conflict with one another. To deny a person's reality is to invite psychosis.
     So they had to settle this. Eusebius and the boys had to accommodate all these groups – the groups who thought that Jesus was an experience, those who thought Jesus a real person, and those who considered him both. This is what the Trinity is all about. This was necessary to accommodate everyone. They make Jesus a real person, as well as God and the Holy Ghost, and eventually, he shows his face. That, to me, is how we go from an experience with these substances to Jesus as a real person. Pure politics.
     Then, what we see within that time frame is that the groups that survived did something very smart. They started to ordain people to commune with the deity and the rest of the congregation was out. At the time of John the Baptist, or whoever it may have been, you didn't have any priests. Because once you have a hierarchy, then you have a political structure. You wouldn't have had anything like that

at John the Baptist's time.   But as time goes on, these groups restricted access to the experience to special people, and these are the ones who became the priests.   And once you restrict this to special people, the knowledge disappears.   It doesn't take long – a couple generations and then people have forgotten about it.   Of course they have their beer and their wine and their cannabis and so on that they're using, but the other substances are secret.   Now, the other Pagan groups roaming around at this time were certainly using beer and wine and probably cannabis, and probably some of these substances as well.   But their goals were a little more group oriented rather than individual/experiential.   So they probably were not in large measure using a lot of these substances.   They were at certain levels, for example, the mystery cults, but not the average person.   Most people were poor and the poor don't having bathing privileges at the Mithras' temple down the street.

So as time goes on, the knowledge of these substances is restricted.   But there is knowledge within the church that their god is a mushroom, and that knowledge is there to this day.   Why? Because if you change the symbols, the rituals connected to them lose their power, and the original rituals were all about the mushroom.

Let me read you something.   This comes from the *Encyclopedia of Christianity*, edited by John Boden, 2005, and there's a wonderful little article here on icons.   It's written by Keith Walker, formerly Residentiary Canon at Westminster in England.   He says here: "Icon painting is a canonical art.   In other words, it manifests the dogma and teaching of the Orthodox Church.   Thus the icon painter is an obedient servant of the Church and it is the Church that authorizes his work.   It is also insisted that the icon painter must be a believer leading a prayerful and Christian life.   The truth of Christianity lies, for the Orthodox, partly in what the Church teaches, but also in the illumination given to those open to the activity of the Holy Spirit. These two witnesses support each other and always agree. There is a tradition that the image of the subject to be rendered externally as an icon *must appear first in the painter's heart*.   This appearance is understood as God's gift completing human endeavour. I remember commissioning Sergei Fyodorov, on behalf of the Chapter of Winchester Cathedral, to paint an icon of St. Swithun, patron saint of the cathedral and perhaps never painted as an icon before.   I supplied the little historical information we have of the saints' life. The icon did not appear. After conversation I supplied information about the holy legend of the saint. The imaginative and ecclesiastical perceptions of Fyodorov were released, met by the inspiration of God. The image appeared in his heart and the icon was completed in about a month."

The story Rev. Walker told Fyodorov was of the Seven Sleepers, who went to sleep in a cave after eating some interesting food, only to be awakened many years later (see *The Golden Legends*).   Now, what does Walker mean by his comments? What lies under all this? I've been attempting to contact Rev. Walker but with no luck, although I have spoken to many others, including a famous icon artist, as she agrees that the mushrooms are in the art, although she claims to not understand what they mean. I have much more to say about guilds, art associations, and artists in *The Mushroom in Christian Art*.

MB – So let's step back here. We've got the people doing the paintings, creating these images, and we could then also include the people doing the architecture in the cathedrals and the basilicas – who are these people and do you surmise that they know the truth of what they are doing? Are the guild members ignorant or initiated?

JR – Initiated. I'm sure they're initiated and they know all about this. It's secret and they're licensed, to this day. You see, these images need to be repaired and you have to get close to them. Artists would see these things, and the artists are controlled by the Church.

I've put out emails to different art associations about this question and no one will talk to me until recently. No information *is* information and it's telling us that something's going on here.

Guilds are very important in this. There were major guilds in Florence in the late Middle Ages and Renaissance, and one of these guilds was the Guild of Physicians and Pharmacists. This is the guild that these artists belong to. The physicians and the pharmacists don't have the proprietary drugs like they do today. They're not making this stuff in a lab. They're going out and pulling up herbs and taking bark off of trees, digging up roots, etc., to make their pharmaceutical substances. The artists would have known all about this and all these substances because they are using plants and minerals as colors in their artwork. I'm also sure that the artists used these substances as well; they imbue these images with power by manipulating lines, shades, and colors in order to bring the past into the future in its same form and function. Shamans all!

Looking further back in time, in ancient Egypt, the artists belonged to the House of Life (*per ankh*), which was also manned by the physicians. So, the artists and physicians way back in ancient Egypt, in 2000 BCE, had their own special guilds. These guilds were overseen by the priests. This is where the secret knowledge was kept.

These guilds we find in Florence were also overseen by the Church, just as the priests in Egypt oversaw the guilds there. They would have known about these substances that are being kept secret from the general public. They would have indoctrinated the people who were doing this art. They had to be true believers, if you will, and they had to keep their mouths shut about certain things, especially about the mushroom.

I should mention that I think the image of the mushroom is somewhat generic and representative of sacred substances in general. You see, not everyone is an amanita person. No everyone is a henbane person. So they have a variety of things, and not only that, but they're combining them and certain substances were probably seasonal.

MB – So the amanita is an icon. It's a representation of all of these kinds of medicines and it's not just particularly the amanita that they're using or considering to be sacred.

JR – What Joseph Campbell said was that this is the transformation of myth through time. We see that mushroom all over the place. We find it in kids' storybooks and Mario Bros and on down the line. I've got all kinds of these things around the house. Every time my wife goes out shopping and finds something featuring an amanita, she brings it home. These things are everywhere and we can find them down through history. Their context and meaning changes over time, but there's a real history there. You can still pick up within these images their significance through time. But again, if you deny the existence of these substances or you restrict it to a special group, the average person doesn't get it or understand it – wouldn't even see it.

I've shown my students images, flashing them up on the screen, and I'll ask, "Do you see the mushrooms?" They say, "No."

Then I point them out and they say, "Oh yeah! Not only that, but there's one over there, etc." So once you point out where these things are in the image, how to find them, and what they look like, then you start to notice them and actually see a mushroom typology. I should caution that some are problematic at best, and you have to be careful. You can Gestalt mushrooms from anything. But on the other hand, there are things there that are obviously mushrooms and there isn't any misinterpretation involved.

Why are they there?

There's nothing accidental in any of these mosaics or stained glass windows. The mushrooms were featured intentionally. They are there for a reason, and it isn't trivial.

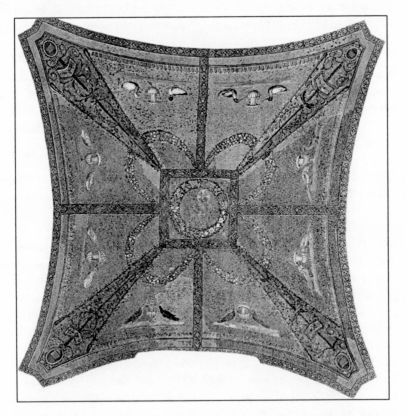

Pairs of birds face red and white *amanita* mushrooms in this baptismal dome

When inspected in detail, the *amanita* appears to rise from a cup. Dr. Rush adds: The mushroom in the chalice is most likely a play on the Book of the Dead, where, in Gate Five (see *The Twelve Gates*), we see the ben-ben stone arising out of the primordial sea, and when it enters the field of time it splits in two. Here we see the two wives of Osiris, Isis and Nephthys balanced against the male energy represented by Khepri (another manifestation of Re).

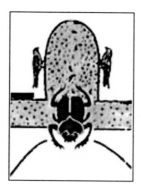

They represent the different aspects of the female energy. Notice in the mosaic the chalice and Amanita muscaria are flanked by birds as well, but this time male and female. The mushroom in the chalice became the cross in the chalice and is a determinative for Gethsemane ("oil press"). – personal email, 2009

MB – So it's not like they're creating these artworks for aesthetic purposes where "we need to put a mushroom here to finish the composition."

JR – They're all there for teaching purposes. People end up worshiping them, but they're there for teaching purposes. What are they really teaching here? Well, that can be learned by looking at these images up close and personal.

So these images are there. They've been there all along, but they haven't been adequately addressed by scholars and academics. But addressing this represents relatively new ground and would overturn a great deal of older scholarship. This presents challenges to young scholars who want to explore this. When you're a graduate student, you don't go to your thesis advisor and call him a fool. You don't tell him he's wrong. You don't do this, because they've got egos, and that can be disastrous for a graduate student. So you go along with what they've said and you don't really pay attention to these details.

Scholars really have not paid attention. I've got books here where people say they've gone over these images with a microscope and so forth. But why didn't they see this? Mushroom symbolism is never mentioned. They didn't know what they were looking for, so they didn't see it.

What I'm doing in the *Mushroom and Christian Art* book is showing people where these things are in the images and a general mushroom typology. What I'm doing is giving my interpretation, which is totally different for many of these images and themes found within popular Christianity. To me, it's a more interesting interpretation. Whether it's exactly right or not, I don't know, but I'm going to put it out there and then the scholars can argue about the details.

MB – Assuming, for the moment, that your general interpretation is correct, how is this going to impact our interpretation of Christianity at the art level, the mythological level, and more broadly than that, what does this possibly mean for Christianity today?

JR – I've had to work on this in my own mind, because this is kind of disturbing. You have the major portion of the world population being Jewish, Christian, or Muslim, and now you're going to turn it upside down.

So I look at it this way: the images can be read spiritually, and it's the spiritual experience that is the core of these traditions, as we can see in the art. Most people, when they go to church, that's not a spiritual experience. They pray for health, wealth, and progeny, your animal nature. There's nothing spiritual in that whatsoever. They're not having genuine spiritual experiences.

MB – No.

JR – So what I'm saying is that these people were having a spiritual experience with these substances and that's what these traditions were about originally. And I can personally attest that these substances can bring the individual to spiritual experiences. I've taken these things. I don't know how many times you have to take them to get the point of it. *Amanita muscaria* I took back in the 70's a couple times and that was enough for me, as I'm not an *Amanita muscaria* person, apparently. Henbane is good.

But most people aren't going to church for a genuine spiritual experience. They're going to church, and they're asking the deity to pay attention to their animal natures. Instead of doing that, why don't you get into a spiritual experience? Just think what would happen to Christianity if they reintroduced the real sacrament to people?

MB – And actually have a spiritual experience rather than just an experience of religion?

JR – Right, and then it becomes a *personal* thing. Then each person can understand the sacred experience for him or herself. You don't need a whole religion for that to take place.

This is why they had to make the storyline connected to Jesus real. If everyone is having their personal experience, you can't organize a religion around that. I've got my own ideas about it and you've got yours and so we're going to be at loggerheads. Making Jesus a real person and centralizing this belief in a powerful church moves us away from the personal experience and into institutionalized religion, which is basically a political structure. I gave a presentation on this idea last fall in August and when I got through I had several people jump up and say, "I want to become a Christian!"

So in my thinking, I'm not sure the Church should necessarily open this experience to everyone. Not everyone is open to working with entheogens. But I think that instead of throwing the whole system out, once you get past this stuff as truth, as historical fact, once you get to the next level, you start to see that really, within all this misery, portrayed on the surface in the Christian art, is a sense of joy and hope. I've played with these pictures now for over eight years, and as I look at them spiritually, there's a lot in there. So we don't need to throw it out. We just need to get away from this idea that it's historical fact.

MB – What kind of impact do you see as this having on society? If we get down to it and claim, "The root of Christianity is actually the consumption psychedelic plants," what does that mean for people like your students who say, "OK. I'd like to be a Christian"? What does that mean for society?

For me, I think that this is exactly what we need. Let's get out of religion and let's get back into personal spiritual experience. That's what I see as the value of entheogens and psychedelics. They allow people to have these experiences without anybody telling them what they're supposed to think or believe or do. And we don't need all the dogma because we have the experience right here.

Obviously, in U.S. law and culture, we don't protect that kind of thing. We protect the institution of religion and one's ability to believe or belong, but we don't protect any kind of spiritual experience at all. Could this, perhaps, initiate a shift and say, "If the core of the religion is actually the experience, then that is what we need to protect. Our rights must include not just our ability to say 'I believe this,' or 'I believe that,' but 'I actually get to do this because this is my tradition.'" Do you see this as contributing to such a shift in our understanding of rights?

JR – I think so. You see, true religion has been outlawed. Christianity doesn't preach religion. Neither does Judaism or Islam. These are political systems, pure and simple. And for scholars to label these as religions is just silly. They're not. Religion was outlawed at least by 560 BCE in the Jewish tradition and by 325 CE by the Church.

You see, what religion really stood for, if we go back to the original definition, was that a person in a religious, spiritual way, identifies with the god. So the god is open: he or she's transparent. You identify with the god, you communicate with the god, and you become the god. That was the original religion, you see. This is personal identification with and experience of the divine.

But Constantine had a problem with all that. You've got people arguing and killing each other over it, so they had to develop a system where these substances were demonized, experiences were limited to certain people, and the individual was forced into a position of worship rather than identification with the deity.

MB – So then it basically became a social and political institution at that point.

JR – And that's exactly what it is today, and it has nothing to do with religion as such, if we define religion as personal experience of and identification with the deity.

In terms of opening this kind of experience up, I think that people can really benefit from it. My experiences with these substances have been very rewarding. There have been several occasions where it's been hell – you often bump into this on belladonna, for example, because of the atropine or whatever else is in it – you can have a really bad time with that. What saves you is the recognition that this is "drug real" and not "real real" and you can wait the whole thing out, or just jump headlong into it.

But overall, I've had some very interesting spiritual experiences with these substances where the general idea comes through: Just be a decent person. And that's all that was said initially anyway. The reason why that didn't stick is because you couldn't sell this idea of being a decent person to the power structure because they weren't decent. They were doing some awful things to people and this would have turned the government upside down. So that message would not have fit at that time period anywhere.

It could fit now. It would definitely fit now. With these substances, the individual could have one of these original kinds of experiences. It would maybe validate that there's another side to our selves, and what we experience as ordinary perception isn't necessarily all there is to be experienced and known. There's a great variety to what one might experience; it places the individual in a personal relationship with the deity *and* more of an appreciation for life.

Now, if you want to sell religion today, that's what you do. You get the person into an individual relationship through these "substances," God if you will, so the individual can identify with, communicate with, and become the god. The churches would be full, get them to pay taxes, and that would solve the budget crisis. The best thing for the Catholic Church to do would be ignore me, if they want to keep this secret. The best thing for the scholars to do is ignore me. I don't think they can at this point because there are too many of us out there now and there are too many books that are coming out. It's inevitable that this information is going to get out and people will have to start talking about it.

In the 1960's you had a resurgence of interest in this. Certainly Leary had a lot to do with it and there were other players in there, Richard Alpert and so on, who were reintroducing these substances to people. The government was scared to death about this because these substances prompt people to think outside their daily routines, and the government didn't want people thinking differently. So they had to close the door on this. You've still have people in jail today for smoking cannabis back in the 60's, which is outrageous. It's ridiculous, totally ridiculous. But it's there. We have these laws. The problem with introducing or reintroducing these substances as a spiritual experience is the government, not necessarily the substances themselves, because the government is scared to death of people thinking in different ways or thinking outside of the box and challenging the politic. This is absurd in today's world.

Also, looking back at the 1960's shows us how Christianity originally developed. In the 60's and 70's and early 80's, you had all these groups, communes full of people having psychedelic experiences, and they branched off and branched off, most disappeared; some are still around. And then you have EST and Scientology (which actually developed back in the 50's), I'm OK, You're OK, Gestalt therapy; all these new and different therapies "mushroomed" out of the 60's "flower power" groups. There were all these people looking for that new workshop that would bring them to illumination. I think you probably had a similar thing back in the time of our mythical hero, Jesus.

You also have a mental health issue here that I tried to point out in the book (*Failed God*). Joseph Campbell came up with this same thing years ago, back in the early 1980's. He said, during the week, we're with Prometheus. We're doing our thing, we're self-responsible. We get up in the morning, we go to work, we do our jobs, or whatever. Then for an hour or so on Saturday or Sunday, we're with the deity, and then on Monday morning we're on the psychiatrist's couch trying to figure this whole damn thing out. We go from the realities of everyday life and then go to church, temple, or mosque, and engage a purely make believe world, out of touch with the time, and then try and bring ourselves back to reality. This psychic split is not insignificant because the brain is attempting to accommodate two entirely different realities; confused realities is part of the definition of neurosis and psychosis

See, this is the problem with this in today's world. This myth, the Christian myth, does not fit in today's scientific world. It would have fit 2,000 years ago, but it doesn't fit now. So this leads to a great deal of anxiety. It leads to a great deal of confusion. It leads to mental health problems. So we've got a wonderful set-up, I suppose, for the psychiatric community with all this. I think that there is an issue here of going from this magical, fantasy world of Jesus dying and resurrecting and all that mythical thinking to the real world of the individual who gets up and goes to work and leads a very ordinary, non-magical life, where people don't arise from the dead or walk on water. Living in these two mind-sets, the mythic and the everyday world, is incongruent. They are not compatible.

And this leads to a great deal of emotional problems. I've been a therapist for years. I've been in private practice since the 1970's and though I don't run into it every day, you certainly do run into it in families where the wife, for example, wants to go to church and you have the husband saying, "that's a bunch of nonsense!" This creates conflict in a family. And then of course the wife goes to the pastor, and he says, "Well, bring the husband into the church, that'll solve the problem." Well, maybe it does, maybe it doesn't. I have examples of individuals wanting to leave the church and they have lost custody of their children through efforts of church personnel interceding in the courts. This is especially the case with Jehovah's Witnesses and Seventh Day Adventists.

The other part of this is that many of the Christian groups engage in some pretty unusual behaviors. Just look at Waco Texas back in the 90's with the Branch Davidians and whatever went on there, and this recent thing in El Dorado where they were practicing ritual sex in the temple with a bed next to the pulpit. And we have these mentally challenged older men having sex with these 13, 14 year old girls. I've asked the Mormons about this and they say, "Well we can't be held responsible for this." Of course they can! They are the ones that filled these people's heads with this nonsense to begin with, so they have to take some responsibility. So I see this as a mental health issue as well.

MB – I agree. I think that it really causes problems in contemporary society where we have, on the one hand, our ideas of scientific truth and everyday reality, and then on the other hand, we're fed this irrational, mythological, basically fantasy thinking that we're told we're supposed to take as literally true, or at least true at some level.

But missing from all that is any kind of personal experience of the sacred or the divine. When you step into that kind of experience, what comes out is that it is an experience of radical freedom and radical responsibility and that we've got to make our own choices. It's not about just believing something.

But when it comes to the politics of truth and belief, we do not know how to operate as spiritual beings living in the modern world because we're completely fractured on all of these fronts of who we are and how we understand ourselves in relationship to whatever it is we conceive as the sacred.

JR – We need to grow up. Huston Smith said it just right. He said, if you're going to enter into these substances, you're going to enter into another level of personal responsibility with them. And the deeper you go, the deeper the responsibility you must assume. That, to me, is an important statement, because what's lacking in this world is personal responsibility.

You can see it in the language - people believing that other people give them emotions. Men in the Muslim community believe that women give them erections. That assigns a tremendous amount of power to the woman. Then she becomes feared, and you've got to dress her up from head to toe. I had one of my Muslim students telling me the other day that this is why in the mosque the men are always up front praying and the women are always in the back. The men get too excited when the women are praying – you can get the image there.

This type of irresponsibility probably came out of the Middle East with the idea that the god was responsible for everything. Nebuchadnezzar gets a set of rules from the sun god, or Moses gets a set of rules from his deity. They don't claim to make up the rules. The rules come from a higher source so they cannot be argued with. This is what's called the third person approach. You win a battle; you attribute the win to the god. You lose a battle; you attribute the loss to the god. You kill somebody because you don't like them; you attribute it to the god. Everything is attributed to this third person out there and that's tremendously emotionally and socially irresponsible – there's no other way to express it. And you see this everywhere. I haven't been able to find a language in the world where the speakers consistently take responsibility for their feelings. We see this in English when people say, "You make me angry," or "You piss me off," or "You make me frustrated," or "It made me angry" or "It interested me." That's all emotional irresponsibility.

MB – Rather than owning it and saying, "I am feeling angry toward you because I've chosen to interpret your activity this way and react in this way."

JR – Right, and it isn't just a word play. There is a different reality created. If I say, "You're making me angry," I'm going to get a defensive reaction from you. If I say, "I'm angry," you're probably going to get curious and say, "What's wrong?" And then I can tell you.

The Sapir-Whorf hypothesis of language investigates how language creates reality. There are some problems with it, but there is some great truth to this. The incantations that you put out there, in your own mind, have a reality to them, and are going to be taken in a particular way by the receiver. So the way you put words together becomes very important in terms of how you relate to everyone or everything in your world. And if you believe that other people give you emotions, my god, you're trapped in jail! You're stuck.

MB – And then you're also absolving yourself from your responsibility for who you are and how you're carrying yourself in the world. You can say, "Everything is impinging upon me from outside!" But again, getting back to the experience of psychedelics and entheogens, it's pretty clear to me that they are saying, "You are 100% completely responsible for yourself, so you've got to own that." And you can't put that off on anybody else or any deity or god, or anything else. It's up to you as an individual.

JR – As we look at the political systems around the world, and certainly we can look at Christianity as a political system, we're in a world community now. You can't control everybody. You can't monitor everybody. These systems like socialism and communism and Marxism don't work. And the reason they don't work is they don't match our human nature.

Back in 1996, I wrote *Clinical Anthropology*, and in that I defined humans as an animal and what the components were: We're a small group animal. We get engaged in analogous thinking. We're dualistic, and so on. And for us, for a small group animal, we don't work well in an urban setting. We ignore most people. If you talked to every person you met when you walked down the street, you'd never finish your journey. You'd never get anywhere. So you have to ignore everybody.

In a system like this, when you have political systems that are telling you "thou shalt not" and there are all these rules, these systems implode from the inside because you spend most of your time and energy policing people. You can't control everyone all the time so it creates tremendous social pressures and problems. Then outside groups can enter in and destroy the whole thing, exploiting the dissatisfaction that already exists.

What we need to build here, which I think comes out of my study of this, is a self-responsible individual who understands emotional responsibility and can then work within this system as a self-responsible individual. Without emotional responsibility, you can't get there.

MB – And really, that is the path to true freedom: People taking responsibility for themselves. Not relying on other people to tell them what to think or do or believe, but everyone takes individual responsibility. That is a free society.

JR – Freedom is not the government doing things for you. That's not what freedom is at all. As a matter of fact, the government would like you on welfare and on prescription drugs. That way they can control you.

Most of these scholars and policy makers don't know the first thing about people. They simply are into some philosophy that they picked up in graduate school and they're running with that and they don't understand what it is that the human animal is all about. A good example of this is the economic mess we are in. You have all these high powered PhDs at the prestigious universities and they don't have a clue or we would have fixed things up. No, the system we live in is so big that no one knows what to do, for no matter what you do, it will have a consequence. Who would have thought that the welfare system, designed to help people get back on their feet, would lead to a system of serial welfare and poverty.

If we really want to understand the human being, we need to look to our origins as a species. We developed in small groups, maybe 25, 30/40 people, and that's it. We lived in these types of groups for millions of years. We're a biological being that clings to life as all other animals do. We eat and have sex to maintain life, and we want to feel important in the group. Now, if you've got a group of 40 people, there are as many statuses as there are people to fill them; everyone is important. People know what their roles are, what is expected of them, and what they are responsible for. In today's society with the way it's set up, personal responsibility is neither promoted nor rewarded. We have an entire system built on lack of personal responsibility with people telling you what to do, what to think, and how to behave. That's not the way the human animal originally developed in these small groups that were composed of responsible individuals. I'm not promoting the "noble savage," but we need to understand our biology before we can understand our sociology.

You're not going to move to the responsible individual with Christianity. You're not going to get it with fundamental Judaism, and certainly it won't show up in Islam. These systems are not invested in personal responsibility, because if you were personally responsible and you could think, you might start to question all this. You might actually get curious. I think it was St. Augustine who said that curiosity was one of the worst temptations in the world. Don't think too deeply into this! They're not promoting curiosity and exploration; they are promoting sheep.

MB – Literally – "the flock."

JR – So, if they're not promoting responsibility, then how do we get there? Well, we have to do something pretty radical. I think that *Failed God* is pretty radical, for me to put myself out there like this with this book. You can certainly argue some of the details in the book, but I think the overall message is that we know how these systems started. The story line for them cannot possibly be true, and I want the Catholic Church to explain these mushrooms! What do they mean? Why are they here? And I want the academic community and the art historians involved in this too. How did you miss these things?

MB – I've got to say, I'm really looking forward to reading your book. And even more than that, I'm looking forward to the reaction it's going to get and the response. I really want to hear what the Church as to say about this. And I want to hear what other scholars have to say about this after being presented with this kind of evidence and argumentation.

JR – There are some other things that need to be done. Jan Irvin and I are working on a couple things. I want to get some T-shirts out there, like one with a mushroom on it and underneath "I found Esau" – now most people don't know who Esau is, so you're not going to get beat up [Esau is Semitic for Jesus] – people in the Church would catch on to it. But this image and this idea has to be presented to the public. It's got to get out there. More people need to hear and see this.

If we want personal freedom, and create a world of decency, then we need to change. Certainly our current religions are not accomplishing this. Islam is probably the most intolerant of all these traditions. There are a lot of Muslims who are wonderful, nice people, who want to get out of this. You see, once you get into Islam, you can't get out. It's literally a death sentence. Death is the punishment for conversion. Talk about lack of personal freedom!

Islam also has institutionalized lying, institutionalized revenge, and institutionalized slavery. This is pure and simple a political system. It is not a system of spirituality. Now there are Sufi mystics, but that's a different thing than political Islamism, though certainly Sufis have lead war parties, so they're not totally off the hook.   But these systems do not support the idea of personal responsibility.   How are you going to end up with a decent world if they're not promoting personal responsibility?   If they promote personal responsibility, then their traditions go down the drain, so you can see the bind they're in.   Look at what's invested in all this.   Look at the churches and the mosques and all the art and the gowns and the ideologies and all this.   What do you do with all this?   Do you put it into a museum?

MB – That wouldn't be a bad idea.

JR – Well, I think the Vatican has already prepared itself for this. Have you ever been to the Vatican museum?   It's beautiful.   They've got artifacts in there from all over.   But there's hypocrisy there.   The day we visited the Vatican museum, an article came out in one of their papers, and it came out in the mainstream news as well and even the Italian government was involved.   They wanted all the countries that had looted Italy to bring back all their art and their statues and everything.   But then you walk around in their museum and they have artifacts from Egypt, Turkey, and China and other areas, they've stolen from everybody else.   So, I guess one person's religion is another person's museum piece.

I don't have much hope that the Church will clean up their act on their own.   I don't have a lot of hope that the Islamic community is going to clean up their act either.   Now, let me make a clear distinction. Islam is a political system, a theocracy. A Muslim is a follower of Islam, and just like Christians and Jews are followers of those traditions, there are many types, some true believers and others think it is silly. In any case, the historians are playing right into this thing; they need to address the historical origins of these religions so we can get past the myths. Origins center on these mind-altering substances and the rites and rituals to explain the experiences they provide. There's no historical visibility for Mohammed, for example. None! But you read in the textbooks that he was born at this time and died at this time and went around spreading the word after he talked to Gabriel in a cave! But the problem is that it isn't true. There was probably some general at that time who may fit the role, but he certainly wasn't interested in spreading religion.   He was interested in kicking the Jews, Christians, and others out of Saudi Arabia. They were having a good time of it, they came all the way into Egypt, but they weren't selling religion. This tradition did not start as a religion of conquest.

As a matter of fact, you can see this with the pilgrims who are going to Jerusalem. Supposedly Mohammed died in 632 CE and the Mohammedians (not Muslims) come into Jerusalem around 638 CE. But they didn't condemn the Christians or prevent them from coming into Jerusalem to pay homage to our mythic hero Jesus. This was not a sacred place to them, not whatsoever, at least not at that time. All they did was charge the tourists coming in there a fee. They have this land now and here's a way to make some money, so you're going have to get in line and get your ticket. This is where the stories in the Qur'an came from, by listening to tourist and their stories, and being good businessmen they began to add on and delete and pretty soon, around 750 CE the Qur'an was born.

When the Ottoman Turks come in there, now they've got the Qur'an, and they have their spin on it. They storm in and start persecuting people. So that early group that was going around doing the conquering with Mohammed, or whoever it was, weren't interested in spreading religion. That's all made up. That's all fantasy. They were interested in control.

There's no evidence of anything called the Qur'an until the 8th century; Hadith were put out there to clarify things. What's interesting—I mention this in *Failed God*, is that there are two types of Hadith; ones that are acceptable, and those that are not. The stuff that's not acceptable is simply there to give you the impression that there must have been something real, real stuff, written way back in time, and the scholars, bless their souls, are able to say which are true and which are fakes. But it is all a trick; they're all constructions. It's a literary technique.

Now, the original Mohammed was probably a pretty decent person. He didn't assassinate people; life was personal to him. You can't build trust assassinating people and getting rid of your competition that way. You can't do stuff like that. He was probably a shamanic individual, but not interested in curing, because his god wouldn't have been Allah to begin with, but il Liah, who was the moon god of war. That would be the main deity. Obviously, if he was a caravan leader, he would have gone into Persia and known about these substances. The Arabs had these substances too. There are many mind-altering substances available in that area or through trade. So, he was like a shaman, communicating with the deity, to get instruction from a third person more powerful than he, as a means of bringing his men to action. He was probably a clever person. They were winning wars, and people joined him. Now, as far and converting people to Islam at the point of a sword, that is totally ridiculous; he never did that. He probably said, "Join me and I won't kill you." It wasn't "Join Allah and I won't kill you." People said, "OK. You're winning wars and I want to be on your side; sign me up." And so they joined him, and that's how this whole thing got started. You don't have anything called a Qur'an until much later. They've got this story about Usman burning books to develop conformity, but that's just there to make you say, "Oh, he did a horrible thing, so it must be real." There weren't any books to burn!

MB – I think that all of this is a radical reassessment of all of this history and I'm really excited to see this work getting out there and am very grateful for what you're doing. People need to know this. Especially when confronted with the art and the images, you can't deny it. I'm here looking at your book cover again and there's Jesus, there are the mushrooms, there are Adam and Eve. You can't deny it. So let's deal with it. Let's talk about it openly, and let's reassess society, religion and politics. We're obviously not doing a very good job with the current the state of the world, so let's reassess all of this and get rid of what we need to get rid of and get back to the truth of personal freedom and personal responsibility. Let's make some changes.

JR – I totally agree with you with all of this. We'll see where all this goes.

SALVIA DIVINORUM FROM A-Z

An entheoglogue with

Daniel Siebert

Daniel Siebert runs the Salvia Divinorum Research and Information Center at www.sagewisdom.org. Siebert has been a primary source for disseminating scientifically accurate information regarding *Salvia divinorum* and has been highly influential in making salvia available outside of its indigenous home of the Mazatec region of Mexico. In this interview Siebert discusses the botany, ethnobotany, and indigenous use of salvia, as well as how salvia was introduced to the West and its spiritual and pharmacological properties. This interview is also featured in *Shaman's Drum* magazine, 2009, issue #79.

Martin Ball – It's an honor to talk with you about Salvia divinorum. *You are closely associated with salvia, and your website, sagewisdom.org, offers a wealth of information about this plant. Would you start by telling us a little about where* Salvia divinorum *comes from?*

Daniel Siebert – I'd be happy to. *Salvia divinorum* is a vision-inducing herb traditionally cultivated and used by the Mazatec Indians, who live in the northeast corner of the state of Oaxaca, Mexico. This species has not been found growing outside of the Mazatec region; however, we don't know if it is actually indigenous there. No definitively wild populations have been identified. It appears that all the plants growing in the region are cultivated or can reasonably be supposed to be feral remnants of plants that were once cultivated.

MB – Don't the Mazatecs live in a really wet environment that is conducive to growing salvia?

Siebert – The Mazatecs inhabit varied terrain with diverse microclimates. Most of the Mazatec region is mountainous, and much of that is covered with high-elevation cloud forest. However, the western part of the Mazatec region, in the Teohuacan valley, is an extremely dry, cactus-laden desert, and the eastern side of the Mazatec region, bordering the state of Veracruz, is predominantly tropical lowland forest.

    Salvia divinorum is a moisture-loving plant. Many people who know about the Mazatecs have read about their use of psilocybin mushrooms, and most of the literature talks about the mountainous area around the town of Huautla de Jiménez, which is the economic center of the Mazatec region. Because clouds linger on the mountain peaks, it's constantly moist up there, making that area very conducive to the growth of both magic mushrooms and salvia.

MB – Are you saying that we don't know whether Salvia divinorum originally came from this area, or if the Mazatecs brought it from elsewhere and began cultivating it there?

DS – No one really knows where *Salvia divinorum*, as a species, originated or what its native range actually is. Most populations are clearly under cultivation. There are some that appear to be growing wildly, but they may just be feral remnants of plants that were once cultivated. So far, botanists have only found salvia growing in close proximity to roads and trails, or near villages, farms, and coffee plantations.

A healthy young *Salvia divinorum* plant

Because *Salvia divinorum* plants have weak stems, heavy winds or rain often knock them over. When a stem falls over, roots form where it touches the ground and new shoots grow from the leaf nodes. In a wet environment, such as the Mazatec highlands, the plant spreads very easily in this way. Once plants have been deliberately planted in one area, and if they have adequate moisture and shade, they will spread into surrounding areas. Before long, they will resemble a wild patch of plants, so it's hard to tell whether a plant was deliberately cultivated in an area at some point in the past. The fact that these plants almost never produce seeds is one reason I suspect that they are not truly wild. Most wild plants produce seeds freely, because sexual reproduction promotes genetic diversity, which helps ensure survival. The fact that salvia does not appear to grow wild in the Mazatec region suggests that it may have been introduced from some other region at some point in the distant past.

Salvia exhibits some of the characteristics that one would expect from a plant that has been removed from a wild population. We don't know for certain that this is what happened, but it is a real possibility. When you remove an individual plant from its natural habitat and replant it elsewhere, that plant is no longer able to mix its genes with other individuals of the species. If the plant is self-fertile, it may be able to produce seeds, but repeated self-fertilization often causes inbreeding depression, a condition that can eventually interfere with the ability of later generations to produce seeds.

Salvia leaves usually grow in pairs, but on occasion, can split into threes. The plant will eventually revert back to pairs of leaves as the triplet will only persist for the growth of a few sections of the stem.

Given that *Salvia divinorum* is an important sacramental plant to the Mazatecs, it is quite conceivable that it was transported to the region by the early people who settled there, or that it was obtained through trade with another tribe. So far, it is only known in the Mazatec region, but it could have come from some other area of Mexico or possibly from South America, at some point in the distant past.

MB – Does the fact that salvia rarely produces seed mean that virtually all the salvia being marketed today comes from genetically identical clones?

DS – Yes, that appears to be the case. I can't really say that conclusively because there hasn't been a lot of genetic testing done on *Salvia divinorum* plants. But we do know that salvia is almost always propagated from cuttings, which is a method for producing identical clones. Most of the plants found today around the world are probably genetically identical to plants brought out of the Mazatec region in

1962 by Sterling Bunnell. Since that time, there have been several other collections made of live plants from the Mazatec region, and some have been distributed by commercial nurseries, but even these may be genetically identical to the 'Bunnell' strain. It would be really interesting to collect plants throughout the Mazatec region and do DNA fingerprinting to see if there are any differences between different plants growing in different areas there.

A single salvia plant, such as this, can have several main stalks.

MB – I understand that you have visited the Mazatecs and talked with their curanderos about salvia. What can you tell us about how it is used within the Mazatec culture?

DS – I've been to the Mazatec region twice, but I made the first trip before I knew much about salvia and before I had tried it. My second visit took place after I had begun working on a book about *Salvia divinorum*, and I went there expressly to do research for the book, taking photographs and conducting interviews. On that trip, I learned a lot about salvia, its traditional uses, and some of the mythology surrounding it.

MB – What can you share with us about the traditions and mythology surrounding it?

DS – I found that the Mazatecs use salvia in ceremonies whose format closely parallels that of their mushroom *veladas*. But, there are some differences. It's hard to make generalizations when talking about these things because different Mazatec shamans have different ways of practicing their art. Generally speaking, Mazatec shamans are very secretive about their knowledge, and they often question the views of other shamans in the community—partly to elevate their own status.

The Mazatec people were converted to Catholicism hundreds of years ago, and Catholic iconography and beliefs play a big role in their ceremonial use of mind-altering plants and fungi. The Mazatecs still retain a lot of their ancient, traditional shamanic practices and animistic beliefs, but the ceremonies are colored pretty heavily with Catholicism.

Mazatec rituals that involve the use of mushrooms, salvia, or other sacred plants, are deeply religious events. In my experience, the rituals are directed at contacting very specific supernatural or divine beings in order to obtain help. In the case of salvia, the Mazatecs see the sacrament as an incarnation of the Virgin Mary, or some more ancient feminine entity represented now by the Virgin Mary, and they often seek aid specifically from her or hope for a vision in which she will come to them and give them guidance with the problem at hand. Normally, they only take salvia when they need help with a fairly serious problem; they never take it in a frivolous manner.

Occasionally, they may take low doses of salvia as a remedial medicinal. Reportedly, it is effective in treating physiological problems such as arthritis and headaches, and in regulating some eliminatory functions such as bowel movements and urination. But when used in that way, it is taken in sub-visionary doses. Salvia is taken in vision-producing doses only in ceremonial contexts to address serious problems.

Mazatec people tend to be very superstitious. They often attribute the causes of disease and problems—things like a bad corn crop or trouble in a marriage, which we might attribute to bad luck—to supernatural influences. Of course, they wouldn't use the term *superstitious*. They believe that these conditions are caused by real forces that exist in the unseen realms surrounding them all the time.

When they experience illnesses or problems that they suspect might be caused by some supernatural source or some immaterial influence, they often go to a shaman. Occasionally, the shaman will advise them to take a vision-inducing herb so that they can get in touch with the supernatural realm and seek assistance from various supernatural beings, who may be Catholic entities (such as the Virgin Mary), elf-like beings that live in the forest, or certain other divine beings that they regard as being helpful for particular problems. They use mushrooms, salvia, morning glory seeds, and tobacco as tools for gaining access to the spirit world so that they can obtain help with the problem at hand.

MB – Are salvia and mushrooms used interchangeably, or does it depend on the shaman or the time of year?

DS – It depends primarily on the shaman. In the highlands, the mushrooms are most abundant in the late summer months, the rainiest months of the year, and there are periods when they are not available. Some ethnobotanists have reported that Mazatec shamans use *Salvia divinorum* as an alternative to mushrooms when they are out of season. However, there are some shamans who prefer using *Salvia divinorum* and don't use mushrooms. Some shamans prefer mushrooms and will use salvia only as an alternative when the mushrooms aren't available. There are other shamans who use both and have equal respect for both.

In the past, Mazatec shamans never used dried mushrooms; they only used fresh ones. It was only after outsiders began visiting the Mazatec region, seeking mushroom experiences, that the Mazatecs began to preserve the mushrooms by drying them, so that they could be used throughout the year. But still, fresh mushrooms are preferred.

Up until fairly recently, it wasn't easy to get from village to village in the Mazatec region, and it wasn't feasible to transport fresh mushrooms from other areas. Dirt trails were the only way to get around. Merchants might travel from village to village, but most people rarely traveled to different parts of the Mazatec region. The substantial regional differences in Mazatec language are evidence of the historical isolation of Mazatec communities. Transportation has improved dramatically in the last thirty years. It's still a remote area, but now there are many paved roads and buses; travel is much easier for the Mazatec people. In the past, Mazatec shamans could only use local species of mushrooms. Now, when the mushrooms are out of season in the highlands, they can obtain fresh mushrooms from the tropical lowlands in the east, where *Psilocybe cubensis* mushrooms grow almost year round.

MB – I have found that psilocybin mushroom experiences tend to last much longer than salvia experiences. Does that have an impact on the way the Mazatecs conduct their salvia ceremonies?

DS – It does, to some extent. A lot of Westerners get the impression that salvia experiences are extremely brief, because they are smoking the leaves—and those effects are only strong for five to ten minutes, and are completely over after half an hour. But the Mazatecs don't smoke the leaves; they take them orally, and that produces a more extended experience.

When salvia leaves are ingested in the traditional manner, the experience is typically strong for an hour or so, and then tapers off over another couple of hours. Granted, that's still relatively brief, compared to mushrooms and many other hallucinogenic substances. In contrast to a mushroom ceremony that might last a total of six hours, most salvia ceremonies tend to take about three hours. So the salvia experience is shorter than the mushroom experience, but it is still long enough to enable people to work with it and get some things accomplished.

Some shamans say they prefer mushrooms to salvia because mushrooms tend to work more reliably. This isn't to say that salvia doesn't work well or isn't effective. People do vary in sensitivity to mushrooms, but a moderate dose of mushrooms will generally produce a definite effect for most people. In contrast, people vary quite a lot in sensitivity to salvia. While some people are very sensitive to salvia, others may feel almost no effects even when they eat a lot of leaves. Smoking salvia provides more reliable results, but the Mazatecs only take the leaves orally, so the effects can be a bit unreliable. However, in Mazatec healing traditions, the power to heal and obtain knowledge comes from the spirits invoked in the ceremony. Many Mazatec shamans don't use any mind-altering plants, and those shamans who can access the spirit world without the help of the plants are highly respected. Because the power of the ceremony and the power of the shaman play a big part in the work taking place, it doesn't matter so much when the shaman gives salvia to someone and it doesn't have much of an effect on that person. The plant is just a helper, facilitating access to the spirit realms. It's not absolutely necessary.

When mushrooms or salvia are used during ceremonies, the shamans always use tobacco as well. Even though the effects of tobacco aren't as dramatically mind altering as those of salvia or mushrooms, tobacco is regarded as the most important doctor plant. Often the Mazatecs use *piciete*, which is a paste made from fresh tobacco leaves, in their ceremonies. They grind the leaves up with some limestone and occasionally a little garlic, and rub the paste on different parts of the body, usually on the wrists and sometimes on the temples for protection. Sometimes, they rub it on their gums, where it's absorbed directly into the system. It produces a dramatic nicotine effect, which can be uncomfortable for people who aren't used to it. I wouldn't call it hallucinogenic, but it certainly is mind altering.

MB – Keeping in mind that every ceremony is unique, what happens over the course of a typical three-hour salvia ceremony?

DS – Salvia is always taken at night, in darkness. Basically, everyone sits facing an altar, and most of the evening is spent in prayer. The shaman says prayers for protection and blesses the leaves before the participants ingest them. Part of the blessing involves purifying the leaves in copal smoke. Copal is a kind of incense resin that is believed to have purifying properties. Then the participants begin eating the leaves and wait for the effects to begin.

Taking mushrooms is much easier than taking salvia because you can chew the mushrooms and gulp them down pretty quickly. When you use salvia leaves in the traditional fashion, you must patiently chew your way through a fairly large pile of leaves that are very bitter tasting, and it can take fifteen to thirty minutes just to consume them. Because your mouth is constantly full, you can't talk much during that period.

MB – How many leaves make up a typical dose?

DS – That varies a lot. In the literature, very different doses are reported, and that can be confusing. One thing to remember is that salvia leaves vary a great deal in size. But typically, the Mazatecs harvest the large leaves—they don't pick the little baby leaves. A typical, full-grown salvia leaf is about the size of a man's hand. The average dose is probably in the neighborhood of 30 leaves. A commonly reported dose is 26 leaves, or 13 pairs of leaves. The number 13 has cosmological significance to the Mazatecs, and pairs represent the two sexes, male and female. When they combine the idea of pairs with the number 13, they get 26 leaves. Many shamans also measure out doses of mushrooms in pairs. For example, one person may get four pairs, and another person may get six pairs. Not all shamans do this with mushrooms, but most do measure out salvia leaves in pairs. Although 26 leaves is a common number, I've heard of people eating as much as 60 pairs, or 120 leaves.

MB – What happens after they eat the leaves? Do they chant prayers or engage in healing rituals?

DS – Typically, while the *curandero* is measuring the dosage and blessing the leaves, he or she keeps some candles burning at the altar. Often the shaman will conduct a ritual cleansing and purify the individuals in the room as well, blowing tobacco smoke or brushing bundles of fresh herbs over their bodies. While people are chewing the leaves and waiting for the effects to come on, there's often a little light, either from a candle or from the embers used to burn the copal incense. But once the visionary effects start manifesting, the shaman extinguishes all the lights and starts chanting and praying. The rest of the ceremony is conducted in complete darkness, and much of the time is spent in earnest prayer. The prayers are directed at the Virgin Mary, Jesus, and other divine beings, asking for aid and guidance. Sometimes the shaman shifts into poetic chanting, often seeking the assistance of animistic spirits that live in the caves, the streams, or the sky.

I want to emphasize that the Mazatec use of psychedelic plants and fungi is devoutly religious. Depending upon the particular shaman, and the type of help being sought, Mazatecs may seek the aid of a particular saint or a particular nature-dwelling spirit, but whatever they are asking, they remain very serious and sincere. Readers may be familiar with Terence McKenna's accounts of the playful tykes and little elfish beings that appeared in his mushroom visions. This sort of imagery comes up for the Mazatecs as well, but they make a point of not getting distracted by these entities and their antics. They caution participants to stay focused on getting in touch with the Virgin Mary or another divine being, and to avoid wasting energy getting caught up in the distracting psychedelic stuff. When taking salvia or mushrooms, people often experience bouts of uncontrollable laughter. In my experience, this laughter can be quite cathartic. But Mazatec shamans frown upon such behavior and get very stern if you start giggling during a ceremony. They will remind you that you're there for a very specific purpose and that it's counterproductive to fool around and laugh. They regard laughter as disrespectful to the sacred entities being invoked.

MB – Were the ceremonies that you attended successful?

DS – Yes. I definitely think these ceremonies can help people. Participants often claim to see visions of the Virgin Mary and other divinities, and they receive useful information and remedies for their problems. Now, who knows whether they are actually contacting independent, divine beings, or whether they are just accessing some deep, inner part of the psyche that allows useful information to come to the surface. Either way, many people do benefit from these experiences.

MB – In my experience, our use of salvia in this country is quite different. We typically take it to have novel, perhaps mystical, experiences. In contrast, the Mazatecs seem to use it for very specific practical and healing purposes. Do their shamans in training ever use it for spiritual exploration?

DS – I don't know much about the role of spiritual exploration in shamanic apprenticeships per se, but I do know that Mazatec salvia ceremonies are always profoundly spiritual events.

During my last visit, I spent some time with a Mazatec shaman, an elderly woman, who was apprenticing a young man, and I watched them working together in ceremonies. However, I did not learn much about what was involved in the apprentice's training. Certainly, many of the older shamans do try to pass on the knowledge that was imparted to them by their own teachers. Their knowledge about the most effective ways to use psychoactive and medicinal plants probably goes back for many generations. Hundreds of years ago, when people first began to investigate these plants, there was probably a lot of experimentation being done with them, but I don't think there's a lot of experimentation going on today. Long ago, people worked out how to use these plants effectively for specific purposes, and they passed on that knowledge to subsequent generations.

Interestingly, most Mazatecs have never taken salvia or mushrooms. They consider them to be sacred medicines, and have strong taboos against using them inappropriately. They say if you use these substances inappropriately and without the proper rituals, you can go insane. You're also supposed to abstain from any sexual contact and to follow a special diet—avoiding certain foods, including garlic, chilies, and certain spices—for several days before and after a ceremony. In contrast, Westerners frequently experiment with psychedelics just for fun or out of curiosity, and they often do so quite casually.

MB – Is there any specific rationale given for avoiding these taboo foods?

DS – The Mazatecs regard foods as having hot, cold, or neutral properties. I'm not exactly sure what they mean by those terms, but it might be comparable to the way practitioners of traditional Chinese medicine regard certain herbs as having heating or cooling influences on certain organs. The Mazatecs view different foods as having warming or cooling effects on the body, and say that people are supposed to specifically avoid "hot" foods before and after ceremonies.

MB – I've noticed that salvia can make some people feel hot, especially if there's any kind of resistance to its effects. I wonder if that plays into why some of these foods are prohibited during this time.

DS – I don't know. I do find that people vary in their responses to salvia. Some people feel hot or even sweaty during sessions, but others feel cold or get chills. Perhaps 40% of people experience some kind of temperature shift or sensation during salvia experiences.

MB – Today, salvia is being grown and used by people in the West who have had no contact with Mazatec traditions. Can you talk about how salvia came to the West, and what's different, now that it's here?

DS – In 1938 anthropologist Jean Bassett Johnson described a divinatory herb called Hierba María, which was used by Mazatec shamans. Although he did not collect any specimens, we know from his descriptions of its use that he was almost certainly describing *Salvia divinorum*. That is the earliest account of the plant in the scientific literature. The first herbarium specimens of the plant were collected in 1957 by Arturo Gómez-Pompa, a Mexican ethnobotanist. While researching mushroom use among the Mazatecs, he heard about a plant that had similar vision-inducing properties. He collected samples of the plant and determined that it was probably a *Salvia* species. He wasn't able to identify it beyond the genus level because the plants weren't in flower at the time (without flowering specimens, it is often not possible to identify a species). Gómez-Pompa sent some salvia leaves to Ciba, the pharmaceutical company he worked for at the time, and told the company about their traditional use. Apparently, Ciba did some preliminary research on the leaves, but nothing came of it.

In 1962, Gordon Wasson managed to collect flowering specimens of the plant, and it was identified as a new species of *Salvia* by Carl Epling, of the University of California, Los Angeles (UCLA). He named the species *Salvia divinorum*, in reference to its traditional use as a tool for divination. I should mention that there are about nine hundred species of salvia, and *Salvia divinorum* is the only one known to produce visionary effects.

Also in 1962, Sterling Bunnell, a psychiatrist in the San Francisco Bay Area who was researching hallucinogens, traveled to the Mazatec region to collect psilocybin mushroom cultures in order to grow them for use in psychiatric research. He learned about *Salvia divinorum* during his stay there and managed to collect live specimens, which he took back to California. He shared cuttings from those plants with Alexander Shulgin, who was working for Dow Chemical at the time, and also with Carl Epling at UCLA. Cuttings from those plants were later shared with others, but it took many years before they spread very far.

Back in the sixties, *Salvia divinorum* was thought to be a mild hallucinogen that was reportedly only used by the Mazatecs when the mushrooms were out of season. Most reports indicated that the effects of salvia were extremely subtle—so subtle that they would disappear completely in the presence of bright lights or loud noises. Of course, we now know that is not necessarily true. It was also assumed that the active constituent was very fragile and deteriorated when the leaves were dried, and that one had to use fresh leaves in order to obtain any effect at all. Since there were no commercial sources for live plants or leaves, very few people had the opportunity to experiment with it back then.

In the mid-1970s a few specialty mail order nurseries began to sell salvia plants to the public, but they were expensive. The few Westerners who had tried the plant reported that, even when used fresh, the leaves didn't seem to do much. You had to endure the ordeal of eating a pile of very bitter leaves, and then you had to concentrate hard to tell if you were experiencing anything. Not many people thought it was worth the trouble. It wasn't until the early nineties that people learned how to use salvia effectively.

MB – So what changed? How did people figure out that salvia is an extremely powerful plant that produces powerful spiritual experiences?

DS – Well, a number of different things happened, but I like to think that I played a small role in that transition. My first experience with salvia, in which I chewed the leaves in the traditional fashion, made a big impression on me and led me to conduct a lot of experiments with. That was back in the late eighties and early nineties.

MB – Please tell us a little about your experiments.

DS – Sometime in the mid-80s, I purchased a salvia plant from the Redwood City Seed Company, a specialty mail order company that carried a lot of unusual and exotic herbs and medicinal plants. I had noticed in one of their catalogs that they were offering *Salvia divinorum* plants. I had read a little about salvia and knew that it was a putative hallucinogen, but I also had heard that its effects were unimpressive. Still, I loved collecting unusual plants, so I ordered one. When it arrived in the mail, the plant was limp and looked half-dead. I tried to revive it, but within a few days, it was completely dead.

The plant was expensive for me at the time, and I decided not to spend more money buying another one. Then, about a year later, I attended a Terence McKenna lecture in southern California, where I saw a man in the audience carrying a potted *Salvia divinorum* plant. Since I had seen the plant before, I recognized it right away. I walked over to him and said, "I know that plant." Back then, salvia was virtually unknown, so it would be unusual to find someone who recognized it. I told him about my previous experience trying to grow the plant. He had gotten his plant from the same source as I did, but he had better luck with his. He had successfully propagated cuttings from his original plant and had more than he needed, so he decided to bring one to the lecture to share. When we ended our conversation, he broke a branch off and gave it to me.

By the time I got home from the lecture, the cutting was completely wilted and looked like it could not possibly survive. I put the cutting in a glass of water, misted the leaves, and enclosed it in a makeshift humidity tent. Miraculously, it revived, and in a couple of weeks, it formed roots. I potted the cutting, and it grew very quickly. So now, I had this interesting plant with some unusual folkloric history in my collection, but based on everything I had read about it, I wasn't initially interested in trying it myself. I knew that there were a lot of exotic psychoactive plants reportedly used by Indians in shamanic contexts, but many of those plants didn't seem to do much, had unpleasant effects, or were too dangerous to experiment with. It appeared that in some cases, the plants themselves weren't as powerful as the traditional ceremonies surrounding their use. At the time, I had a tiny greenhouse that was only about six feet tall. After about a year, the plant reached the top of the greenhouse and its stems were pushing against the ceiling. It was in the back corner of the greenhouse, where it wasn't getting good air circulation, and it had a bad infestation of scale insects.

So one day, I decided the plant didn't need to be in the greenhouse, and I started to move it outside. When I tilted the pot slightly to pick it up, the plant—which was very tall and spindly—leaned over and snapped off right at ground level. I tried to salvage it by planting a few cuttings, but there was a lot of leaf material that was going to be thrown in the compost bin. I thought it would be a shame to waste all these leaves, so I decided to refrigerate some of them until I could find time to try them. I didn't think to dry them, because at that time people thought the leaves had to be used fresh.

About a week later myself and two friends—my girlfriend at the time and another friend—got together at dusk and chewed the leaves in traditional Mazatec fashion. There was no indication that salvia had any harmful or dangerous effects that we needed to worry about. My main concern was that the leaves would have no effect. I knew of only one report of a Westerner experiencing strong effects from *Salvia divinorum*, and that report came to me secondhand from Kat Harrison, Terence McKenna's ex-wife. She told me that anthropologist Bret Blosser had taken *Salvia divinorum* leaves with a shaman while visiting the Mazatec region, and that he reported having a rather dramatic experience. Since he was the only person I knew of who claimed to have experienced powerful visions with salvia, I decided to ingest the leaves the same way as he did. He had been told to take twenty-six large leaves, roll them into a cylinder, like a cigar, and chew away until he got to the end of it. So, we each ate twenty-six large leaves that evening.

Just about when I got to the end of my bundle of leaves—it must have taken fifteen to twenty minutes of chewing—I felt a slight tingly feeling. It was nothing definite, but I felt I was perceiving things in a slightly different way. I decided to get up and move around to see if I could detect any differences in my sense of perspective or my sense of motion. When I took a few steps, I noticed that objects in the environment had a glow around them. I said, "I'm definitely feeling something."

In reply, one of my companions said, "I don't feel any...." He later told me that he was going to say "anything," but before he got the word out, he fell out of his chair onto the ground and began laughing convulsively. I wasn't affected so strongly, and I was still able to talk, so I asked, "Are you OK? What's going on?" But he couldn't stop laughing long enough to say anything.

It took a couple of minutes before he was able to speak again. When he did speak, he said, "Are you in it?" I said, "In what?" I didn't know what he meant. He just kept repeating, "Are you in it?"

A couple of hours later, after the experience had faded, he explained what he had been trying to say. Apparently, when he had fallen off his chair, he had experienced falling through the earth into an underground cavern. When he had asked, "Are you in it?" he had been referring to this underground place. I hadn't entered a cavern, but at one point I clearly saw childlike beings who inhabited hobbit-like houses that were nestled into the hillsides surrounding the house where we were doing the experiment.

MB – So it definitely affected you?

DS – It was definitely a visionary experience. At the time, what I was seeing appeared to be quite real. It may not have been real in the ordinary sense of the word, but it certainly felt real to me.

We did our session outside on the back porch of a house at the base of some chaparral-covered hills. I knew there was nothing on these hills other than the natural vegetation. But when I looked up at the hills, I saw all these little houses that were nestled into the hillsides, kind of like the hobbit houses in *The Lord of the Rings*. I distinctly saw little lights coming from the windows, and smoke coming from little chimneys. There was this cozy, quaint little community inhabited by peaceful little beings, who were like nature spirits. For some reason, I had never seen them there before, but they seemed as natural as anything I ordinarily experienced.

MB – So this convinced you that salvia was fairly effective.

DS – Yes, definitely. I had an extraordinary visionary experience. It made a big impression on me. One of the things that impressed me about salvia was that the experience seemed completely natural; I didn't feel like I was on a drug. It seemed that salvia simply opened a little window of perception that allowed me to see things that are there all the time, but not normally perceived. I also felt extremely connected with nature. It was a wonderful, very nurturing experience.

The experience left me feeling fascinated and revitalized. I also felt that the duration was perfect. I sometimes find with other psychedelics, such as LSD, that the experience goes on too long. After a few hours with LSD, I often feel like I've gotten the lessons needed and am ready for it to be over, but then it goes on for many more hours and I find myself just rehashing a lot of the same psychological material. The salvia experience lasted an ideal amount of time for me—long enough to have an interesting experience, do some serious contemplation, and obtain useful insights. I also liked the gentle quality of the effects. I felt perfectly fine afterwards. There seemed to be no significant side effects or lingering aftereffects. For me, it seemed like an ideal entheogen.

Although I continued experimenting with chewing the leaves, my subsequent sessions did not produce nearly the same results. I was mystified, and wondered, "Why doesn't this plant work reliably?" In a series of several disappointing experiments, I'd chew my way through big piles of leaves and hardly anything would happen. So I kept trying to find some way to get the salvia to work as well as it had that first time. I wondered if the leaves might vary in potency at different times of year and if the leaves I was using in the subsequent experiments weren't as strong as those I used the first time, so I tried increasing the dose, but it still wasn't working. I reached the point where the volume of leaves became physically prohibitive—I simply couldn't eat a larger dose.

So I decided to try concentrating large volumes of leaves by making extracts, reducing the material down to a volume that could be more easily consumed. I tried several approaches to making extracts, but none of those produced any effect. One thing led to another, and eventually, to make a very long story short, I ended up isolating a pure crystalline compound. My first experiment with it produced an experience that was much more intense than any previous one I'd had with salvia. My previous impression was that salvia could only produce benign, pleasurable, enriching experiences. I had no idea that the psychoactive principle of the plant, which I later identified as salvinorin A, could produce overwhelmingly intense, sometimes frightening, experiences.

MB – Would you describe that experience?

DS – I was trying to make a concentrated crude extract; I had not set out to extract a pure crystalline compound. In the process of making the extract, I noticed that the solution had an odd iridescent quality. I had made extracts from various other medicinal plants over the years, but I had never seen anything like this. It occurred to me that the iridescence might be caused by tiny crystals suspended in the solution. I assumed that the crystals were probably some inorganic mineral salt, and figured that by filtering them out I could make my extract that much more potent.

So I filtered the crystals out, and was about to dump them in the garbage can, when I thought, "Maybe I should test a little of this stuff. It's probably worthless, but just in case, I should test it."

Salvinorin A

I had several reasons for thinking that it wouldn't be psychoactive, but I cautiously proceeded. I placed a couple of milligrams of it on a piece of aluminum foil, vaporized it by heating the foil from below, and inhaled the vapor through a little glass tube.

Just as I began to think, "Sure enough, this isn't going to do anything," I suddenly lost physical awareness, although I remained conscious. I seemed to be a disembodied consciousness floating around in an immaterial realm. Things were changing very quickly, and I had very little sense of what was going on or how I had gotten there. I had no memory of having made an extract of a plant and having smoked it. That was all gone.

I had the nagging feeling that I was supposed to be someplace other than in this disembodied space, but I couldn't remember where or what that place was. I kept searching my memory, wondering, "Where am I supposed to be?" But I couldn't remember any existence other than the state I was in.

At some point, I concluded that I must have been dreaming that I had come from some other reality, a dream reality that I couldn't quite remember. I surrendered to the idea that I was in the only reality that there ever was, and it was where I was supposed to be. Then I started wondering where I was supposed to go from there. I felt like I was supposed to do something or travel someplace, but I didn't know what or where.

As I was grappling with these confusing thoughts and trying to make sense of it all, I suddenly found myself back in my body. I opened my eyes and looked around. I was standing in a room that I recognized, and I knew it was the real world. Initially I felt a sense of tremendous relief, but then I realized that this wasn't my house; it was my maternal grandparents' house—only it looked the way it had during my childhood. I sensed that I had somehow come back out of the disembodied state and reentered my body at the wrong place in time. Instead of returning to where I was supposed to be, I had reentered my life at a point in the past. It was a very frightening experience, because it didn't seem like a memory in any sense. It seemed very real and solid, and I was terrified. I was thinking, "Something's terribly wrong. I'm not supposed to be here. I can't just start reliving my life from back when I was a little child!"

I was very confused, and I panicked. Somehow, I again lost awareness of my physical existence and reentered a disembodied state. Then it happened again. I suddenly found myself back in a physical place, but it wasn't where I was supposed to be. It was a familiar place, a friend's house. This happened three or four or five times, as I vacillated between experiencing a disembodied state and finding myself in a seemingly real place, only to realize that it wasn't where I was supposed to be. Eventually, of course, I found myself back in my own home at the proper point in time.

When I regained my senses, I was in my house, but I could still feel the effects of the salvinorin A, which were gradually subsiding. In contrast, I had felt completely sober each time that I had been in one of the other places from my past. I've noticed a similar phenomenon with dreams, too, when I have had a few drinks at night and feel inebriated before going to sleep. If I wake up in the middle of the night, I will feel groggy from the alcohol, but in my dreams, I feel completely sober. Apparently, the internal modeling of reality that happens in these visionary states does not often incorporate the feeling that one's state of awareness is altered. Actually, I find a lot of parallels between salvia experiences and sleep dreams. Although they are not identical, both are visionary states of consciousness that can generate extremely realistic imagery, and both often involve familiar places from childhood.

MB – So this was the first time that you extracted salvinorin A and your first experience of it?

DS – Yes, it was. On reflection, that first dose was really too strong. It wasn't a horrible experience and it didn't hurt me in any way, but it was overwhelmingly intense, very confusing, and difficult to make sense of. Since then, I've experienced salvinorin A many times at much lower doses, and at those levels, the experience is much more manageable and friendly.

MB – Can you describe how you began sharing your discovery with other people? What happened then?

DS – Well, I realized that this was an important breakthrough. I had identified the compound that is responsible for the vision-inducing properties of *Salvia divinorum*, and demonstrated that it could be smoked.

Three terpenoid compounds—salvinorin A, salvinorin B, and loliolide—had been isolated from salvia previously, but it was generally assumed that they were not responsible for producing its hallucinogenic effects. Most hallucinogens are alkaloids or alkaloid-like compounds, primarily tryptamines and phenethylamines. The salvinorins had been tested in mice, but not humans. Salvinorin A did cause a "sedative-like" effect in mice, but there was nothing to suggest that it produced the hallucinatory effects ascribed to *Salvia divinorum*.

Now, I had isolated this extraordinarily potent vision-inducing compound but didn't know what it was, so I contacted Jerry Valdéz, one of the chemists who had originally isolated salvinorin A, salvinorin B, and loliolide, and I told him about my experiments. Based on my description of the isolation procedure I had used, he thought that I had probably isolated salvinorin A. He had tested salvinorin A in mice, but he never tested it in humans, primarily because of the academic and ethical restrictions of the university where he was working. Soon after our conversation he sent me a sample of the salvinorin A that he had isolated about ten years previously.

When I received his sample, I did some chemical comparisons (thin layer chromatography, melting point, and NMR spectroscopy), and I found that it was the same compound. As a final test, I self-assayed some of his salvinorin A, and it produced the same effects. That's when I knew that I had isolated salvinorin A and that it was the psychoactive principle of *Salvia divinorum*.

In the following months, I conducted some more experiments taking the leaves orally. I noticed that when I ate the leaves quickly or gulped down puréed leaves, I didn't get any effect. However, when I chewed the leaves for an extended period of time they produced effects quite reliably, even when the leaves were not swallowed. I repeated these experiments with a group of volunteers and obtained consistent results. This implied that salvinorin A was effectively absorbed through the oral mucosa but not through the gastrointestinal system. I hypothesized that salvinorin A was being rendered inactive either by digestive enzymes or possibly by liver enzymes during first-pass metabolism.

When the leaves are taken in the traditional Mazatec fashion, which involves chewing a large pile of leaves, the mouth cavity is continually bathed in leaf juices for a period of fifteen to twenty minutes or so. That allows sufficient time for an active dose of salvinorin A to be absorbed through the oral mucosa. I realized this could be the reason that people outside of the Mazatec region weren't getting much effect from salvia leaves. Because the leaves are bitter tasting, it was common for people to grind them up in a blender with a little water, and then gulp down the slurry quickly to avoid the bitter taste.

Eventually, I wrote a paper describing my experiences with salvinorin A and my finding about the importance of absorption through the oral mucosa. In 1994, the paper was published in the *Journal of Ethnopharmacology*—a scientific journal with a fairly limited academic readership. Soon, the information began to trickle out into the general psychedelic community, and I started getting a lot of mail.

Email was not widely used back then, so people were mostly sending me old-fashioned letters, asking me questions about salvia. They were curious about this new, incredibly potent psychedelic substance, salvinorin A, that reportedly rivaled LSD in potency. There have been a few LSD relatives discovered in recent years that are also extremely potent, but they are all semi-synthetic compounds, like LSD. The fact that salvinorin A occurs in nature and is almost as potent as LSD was big news.

In their letters, a lot of people were asking me many of the same basic, how-to-do-it questions about dosage and methods of use. I was aware of the World Wide Web, which was then still in its infancy, and I thought that it would be a great place to share information about *Salvia divinorum* and provide answers to frequently asked questions. So in 1995 I created a website to share what I had learned about this plant. Then when people contacted me requesting basic information, I simply directed them to my website. That was the origin of the *Salvia divinorum* Research and Information Center website at *sagewisdom.org*.

MB – When did people realize that smoking the leaves was an efficient and effective method for consuming salvia?

DS – In 1975 Jose Luis Díaz, a psychiatrist and ethnobotanist who had been interested in Mexican psychoactive plants for many years and had written a number of papers about them, published a paper in which he mentioned that some urban users smoke the leaves to obtain a mild effect that is inferior to marijuana. He had obtained this information from Jonathan Ott, a pharmacognosist who was studying with Díaz at the National University in Mexico City at the time. Ott did not publish anything about these observations himself until almost two decades later. According to Ott, some students from the university would travel to the Mazatec region on weekends to take mushrooms, and they would sometimes obtain salvia leaves, dry them, and smoke them.

Most people who studied these things dismissed the reports of Mexican college students obtaining effects from dried salvia leaves as being a false rumor, comparable to rumors of people getting high from smoked banana peels. This skepticism was based partly on the fact that Mazatec informants consistently said that the leaves must be used fresh, partly on the fact that an orally active dose was far too large to possibly be smoked, and partly on the fact that two prominent chemists—Albert Hofmann, the discoverer of LSD, and Alexander Shulgin, the creator of many novel psychedelic compounds—each concluded that the psychoactive agent in salvia must be quite labile and probably decomposes when the leaves are dried or processed to make an extract. They had each tested the plant for alkaloids and hadn't found any. They had tried to identify the active constituents in the plant, but neither of them succeeded. Both had tried ingesting extracts from the leaves, and the leaves themselves, but they hadn't found any activity.

About a decade later, during the mid-1980s, American poet Dale Pendell began growing salvia and experimenting with the leaves. Ignoring the prevailing "wisdom" at the time, he dried some leaves and smoked them. He found that the leaves were quite effective when smoked, and later mentioned this to friends. That was several years before I met Dale. Reports of his experiments with smoked leaves came to me secondhand or third hand, and I thought, "Well, maybe he is just one of those people who can get high off of anything." Many other psychedelic researchers, including Terence McKenna, were also skeptical of Pendell's reports at the time. But it turned out that Dale was right.

Eventually, I decided to try smoking the leaves myself. The first time I tried it, I experienced some mild effects. Although the effects were fairly subtle, I was excited to find that smoking the leaves worked at all. This made me realize that the active constituent must be more stable than previously thought, and that encouraged me to continue with my extraction experiments.

I tried smoking the leaves several more times, but all the experiences were brief and relatively mild. Then I gave some leaves to some friends whom I thought might be interested in trying them. About a week later, one of them called me with an astonished tone in his voice. He said, "Those leaves you gave me! That was one of the most incredible things I've ever experienced!" Apparently, he had an extraordinarily intense out-of-body experience after smoking the leaves. Now, this was someone who was very experienced with psychedelics, so I was surprised by his reaction. I was thinking, "Are we talking about the same thing?" This took place before I had isolated salvinorin A and I still thought of salvia as a relatively mild psychedelic. I questioned him and learned that he had smoked the leaves in a different way than I had been smoking them. I had been rolling the leaves in cigarette papers and smoking them like joints, and I had gotten only mild effects. He, on the other hand, assumed that salvia was weak and would require a large dose, so he packed a large bowl full of leaves in a bong and puffed away, taking in as much smoke as he could, and he had this incredibly intense experience.

After hearing about his experience, I got a bong and smoked a bunch of leaves the same way as he had, and sure enough, I had an intense visionary experience. That convinced me that the effects of smoked salvia can be quite powerful, much more so than I had previously thought. The trick is that you need to inhale a lot of smoke fairly quickly to get a strong effect. If you smoke it gradually, like a marijuana joint, passing it around a group or waiting several minutes between drags, the effects don't build up in intensity.

Now that I know more about salvia, it's clear to me that salvinorin A must be metabolized very rapidly in the body. If you inhale some salvia smoke, it starts breaking down within minutes. If you wait too long before taking a second or third hit, the effects won't accumulate. But if you inhale a lot of concentrated smoke in a short period of time, the salvinorin A is able to build up in the bloodstream faster than it is metabolized, and then you experience stronger effects.

Once I realized that smoking salvia works, I got the idea that smoking concentrated extracts of the plant would make it easier to get a full effect without needing to inhale so much smoke. However, I quickly found that smoking too high a dose could produce disorienting and confusing effects, which is something that I never would have anticipated when I first chewed the leaves. It became obvious that salvinorin A is an extremely potent compound and that one needs to be careful to avoid taking excessively large doses. As with all drugs, there's an optimum dosage range that can be used productively.

Unfortunately, the competitive nature of business has motivated salvia vendors to produce and sell ever more concentrated extracts. Many vendors now sell highly concentrated extracts of salvia that are, in my opinion, unsafe for most people to use. If one concentrates an extract too much, it increases the danger that users will accidentally take too large a dose, and that results in people having experiences that are confusing, disorientating, and frightening. Originally, people were selling extracts that were five times more potent than regular salvia leaves (5x extracts). Then some vendor reasoned that they could get more business if they offered something ten times stronger (10x). Soon afterwards, other vendors began offering 15x and 20x extracts. In recent years, I've seen some extracts that claim to be sixty or eighty times stronger than normal potency. To make matters worse, these products are usually sold without any dosage guidelines. Obviously, these vendors do not care about the welfare of their customers. It is a disturbing situation.

MB – How would you describe the salvia experience to someone who has no familiarity with it? What would you tell them to expect?

DS – Salvia produces a unique type of experience, and it's difficult to compare it to other states of consciousness. I have a lot of experience with other mind-altering plants and chemicals, and I find that salvia is totally distinctive.

In a very general way, salvia can be compared with some other vision-inducing substances—perhaps psilocybin, peyote, DMT, and LSD—but only in the sense that they all can generate visionary experiences. However, the quality and character of salvia-induced visionary states are quite different from those produced by other substances.

It's hard to generalize about this because not everyone responds to salvia in the same way. Some people, a small percentage, seem unable to have visionary experiences with it. But for those who do, I would say that salvia visions tend to resemble ordinary sleep dreams more than the visions produced by other hallucinogens. Tryptamine hallucinogens such as psilocybin and DMT, for example, tend to generate complex geometric patterns and bizarre science-fiction-like imagery that often seems very alien and otherworldly. In contrast, salvia tends to produce images that are more familiar. I often see images and scenes from my own childhood. Even when I find myself in places that I don't recognize, there are usually buildings, rivers, and things that resemble the objects I normally encounter in the ordinary world. In that sense, salvia visions are often very similar to sleep dreams.

MB – I understand that salvinorin A is a unique kind of molecule that reacts differently with our receptor sites. Could you tell us a little bit about what it does in the brain?

DS – We now know that salvinorin A activates the kappa-opioid receptor, whereas other hallucinogens, like LSD and DMT, act primarily on serotonin receptors, and secondarily at some other receptors. Salvinorin A is rather interesting in that it binds exclusively to this one particular type of opioid receptor and seems to have no significant activity at any other receptors—at least not any other receptors that have been tested, and it's been tested at over 50 different ones.

There are three main types of opioid receptors: delta, mu, and kappa. A lot of common pharmaceutical painkillers—morphine, codeine, and heroin—primarily exert their effects by activating the mu-opioid receptor, although many also have some secondary activity at delta- and kappa-opioid receptors. Because these opioid drugs are powerful analgesics, they are prescribed extensively for people suffering from chronic pain or recovering from surgery.

The problem with mu-opioid agonist drugs like morphine and codeine is that they are highly addictive and have dangerous and undesirable side effects. People who take them to treat chronic pain develop tolerance to them fairly rapidly and have to keep taking higher doses to maintain an effective level of medication. The most serious danger with these drugs is that they slow respiration, so if you take too much, you can actually stop breathing. The reason that heroin addicts often die accidentally from overdoses is that their breathing stops. Even in hospital settings where these drugs are used routinely to treat post-operative pain, a patient who is unusually sensitive may stop breathing.

Scientists are interested in drugs that work at the kappa-opioid receptor because they can be useful for managing pain without being addictive or slowing respiration. Many kappa-opioid agonist drugs had previously been discovered, but unlike salvinorin A, none of them act solely on this receptor. Some of these drugs have gone to clinical trials, but they have all had unwanted side effects, so they haven't been developed into marketable drugs.

We know that salvinorin A binds to and activates kappa-opioid receptors and we know that this receptor is involved in pain perception. Apparently, the kappa-opioid receptor is also involved in the way that we process perceptions and thoughts, because when salvinorin A stimulates this receptor, it produces profound visionary and mental effects. No doubt we could learn a lot about the mechanics of consciousness by studying how salvinorin A exerts its effects on the mind.

MB – Are you suggesting that salvinorin A be developed into a natural pain-relieving pill?

DS – Possibly. The pain-alleviating properties of salvinorin A have been demonstrated repeatedly in laboratory animals. And the Mazatecs sometimes use low doses of salvia to treat arthritis and headaches, which suggests that it has practical pain-relieving properties. Since salvinorin A works at the kappa-opioid receptor, it makes perfect sense that it would reduce perception of pain.

Pharmacologists are doing a lot of experimentation with salvinorin A and its derivatives, hoping to identify and develop useful medications. Certainly, drugs derived from salvinorin A could be useful for treating pain without producing the unwanted side effects associated with mu-opioid agonist drugs like morphine and many of its derivatives. Obviously, the hallucinogenic effects of salvinorin A would be considered an unwanted side effect in the treatment of pain. However, by modifying its molecular structure, pharmacologists might be able to produce drugs that have useful pain-alleviating properties but don't produce profound alterations of consciousness.

MB – Obviously, conducting that kind of research could be hampered if salvia's legal status were to change. Can you tell us a little bit about what's going on with salvia and the law right now?

DS – Unfortunately, salvia has gotten a lot of negative publicity in recent years. A number of states have banned salvia or passed regulations on its sale. Some of the state laws are quite severe. For example, Oklahoma has a new law that can put a person in prison for up to ten years simply for possessing salvia, and distribution carries a penalty of five years to life. If that is not draconian, I don't know what is. Some other states have more moderate regulations. Maine has a law that prohibits possession by minors; it also makes it illegal for an adult to provide salvia to a minor. California recently enacted a similar law; it makes it a crime to sell salvia to minors but allows possession by minors as well as adults. For the moment, however, salvia is still legal in the majority of states. There is a page on my website with detailed information on the current legal status of salvia in each state, as well as abroad.

The federal government is currently studying salvia, in order to determine whether to ban it or not. It seems to me that, given the growing number of states passing laws against salvia, it may be only a matter of time before it is banned at the federal level. It's anybody's guess as to when that might happen. On the other hand, given that there is no compelling evidence to suggest that *Salvia divinorum* presents a significant risk to public safety, I am hopeful that they will be reasonable and not criminalize this beneficial plant unnecessarily.

MB – What are some of the arguments that are being used to justify banning salvia, other than the fact that it's a visionary plant?

DS – There really isn't any good evidence that salvia is harmful in any significant way, and it's certainly not an addictive substance. In fact, most people who try salvia don't particularly like its effects and don't repeat using it more than a few times, if at all. Certainly, there are some people who think salvia should be banned simply because it has profound mind-altering properties.

Unfortunately, the popular media keeps coming out with stories that exaggerate, sensationalize, and misrepresent salvia's effects. In addition to being compared to LSD and a whole slew of other drugs, saliva is often portrayed as a major threat to the youth of America. When people start hearing that a drug might harm children, that gets their alarm bells ringing. Most efforts to ban salvia seem to be knee-jerk reactions on the part of legislators who feel called upon to protect the population from anything that might potentially be dangerous. Unfortunately, the people who are passing laws banning salvia have never tried it, and they're not well informed about it. They refuse to consider the scientific evidence, which shows that salvia is not addictive and toxicologically harmless. Many people assume it must be dangerous simply because it produces visions, but that's a logical fallacy (a non-sequitur): visionary states are not necessarily dangerous. I like to remind people that sleep also produces visions.

When you look at the actual facts about salvia, you see that there's really no rational reason to ban its use by responsible adults. It is probably one of the safest mind-altering, vision-inducing plants. There is no evidence that salvia causes any serious psychological, physiological, or sociological problems. However, there is plenty of evidence that appropriately informed and prepared adults can and do benefit from using salvia.

I do think it's reasonable to regulate its sale and public use in some rational manner. For example, I don't think it's appropriate to allow children access to salvia, especially not concentrated extracts. The laws passed in Maine and California prohibiting the sale of salvia to minors seem totally appropriate.

In my opinion, this is a human rights issue. We need to recognize that people have a right to explore their own consciousness and delve into their own minds. If a substance is relatively harmless, if it's something that is found in nature, and especially if it has a long history of being used safely in religious and medicinal contexts, I think it's wrong for the government to step in and say, "No, you can't use this."

MB – Since your website is devoted to educating the public about salvia and counteracting misinformation, could you talk about what you offer there?

DS – As I mentioned earlier, the site was originally conceived as an educational resource. Since I had a lot of experience using salvia, had researched it thoroughly, had identified salvinorin A as the psychoactive principle of the plant, and was the first person to perform human experiments with salvinorin A, I felt I had some important information to share. In addition to offering practical advice for people interested in using salvia, the site includes ethnographic reports describing Mazatec usage of the plant and provides detailed information about its botany, chemistry, and pharmacology. It also includes experiential reports and scores of relevant articles from scientific journals.

I have always emphasized the importance of using salvia safely and responsibly. I also emphasize the importance of having a sitter present during the experience, particularly for first time users who have no idea how sensitive they may be to a given dose. Whether or not one decides to use salvia is a decision that each person must make for him or her self. I encourage people to thoroughly educate themselves about salvia before making that decision.

Salvia is an herb that has fascinated me for many years. When used wisely, it can engender extraordinarily rewarding experiences. I plan to continue sharing my findings and providing information so that others may benefit from it in the future.

MB – I would add that you've been very effective in that. I've always been very impressed by sagewisdom.org and the amount of information provided there. My early introduction to salvia was inspired by your site, and it continues to mean a lot to me. For anyone who is interested in working with salvia, I can't recommend it enough—it's definitely the place to go.

ENTHEOGENIC SPIRITUALITY AS A HUMAN RIGHT

Martin W. Ball, Ph.D.

The following essay is an edited excerpt from the book, *The Entheogenic Evolution: Psychedelics, Consciousness and Awakening the Human Spirit* by Martin Ball (Kyandara Publishing, December 2008) and was originally published on Realitysandwich.com.

I'm including this essay here as many of the ideas expressed herein were inspired by the conversations that I had with the individuals featured in this book. With all the evidence of the spiritual nature of entheogens, I strongly feel that the time has come to recognize their intrinsic value. It is also a question of true spiritual freedom for individuals, not just religions. After presenting a history of cultural and legal issues surrounding entheogenic spirituality, this essay concludes with a call for the universal recognition of the human right to entheogens.

The true heart of any religion or spiritual tradition is direct spiritual experience. It is from the immediate experience of the sacred that traditions arise, grow, and take on a life of their own as institutions and systems of belief. Yet without that initial spiritual experience, the inspiration that originally gave rise to the tradition, there is very little to base the tradition upon.

It isn't difficult to see that this basic proposition is true. Of the "great" traditions of the world, meaning the more popular and well-established traditions, we find persons who were deeply immersed in direct spiritual experience. In the Judaic tradition, we find imposing figures such as Moses, who communed with God on the mountaintop, directly receiving messages and instructions from the beyond. Later, in the Christian tradition, we have the figure of Jesus, realizing and experiencing his own divinity. More recently, we find Mohammed in the Islamic tradition with his ecstatic flight to heaven to commune with Allah.

To the East, many more examples abound. In Buddhism we have the mystical figure of the Buddha, enlightened through meditation under the Bodhi tree. In the Taoist tradition, we find the sage of Lao Tzu and his work, the *Tao Te Ching*. The Hindu and Jain traditions also have countless significant mystics and saints, all inspired by their personal enlightenment experiences.

From the direct experiences of mystics, shamans, sages and saints, prophets and holy people, come the teachings and practices that become codified as religious and spiritual traditions and are then taught to others and passed on across cultures and history. But, at the root, at the very heart, we find inspired individuals who glimpsed and felt something of the sacred that impacted upon them so profoundly that they felt compelled to share their experiences and teachings with others, providing them with a path and methodology for experiencing the sacred themselves.

In U.S. law, religion has largely been defined according to the concepts of belief and practice. Coming from the Western and Christian traditions, where belief and right practice of worship have been overwhelmingly emphasized over any form of direct spiritual experience, U.S. law sees "freedom of religion" as referring primarily to the freedom to believe and secondarily to the freedom to practice. According to U.S. law, we are all free to believe whatever we want. No one can force us to believe any particular dogma or religious teaching, and if we choose, we can believe in nothing at all. As for practice, we are free to practice our religions however we see fit, as long as those practices do not interfere with the greater interests of the State, violate laws, or impinge on others' constitutional freedoms and rights.

However, something sorely missing from our legal protections is any recognition of the significance of direct spiritual experience itself. One can believe or practice however one may like, but that does not mean that one will necessarily have any kind of direct spiritual or mystical experience. In fact, given the general spiritual disenchantment currently plaguing the West, it isn't a stretch to say that all our emphasis on correct belief and practice has largely cut us off from any kind of direct spiritual experience, which explains the strong attraction Westerners have to Eastern and Indigenous traditions where the emphasis is on experience. We in the West are largely starving for spiritual experience and a re-enchantment of our experience and view of the world and of ourselves.

Not only have many sought to find this re-enchantment through Eastern and Indigenous traditions, but also through the use of psychedelics and entheogens. However, these agents of spiritual experience and awakening are largely illegal in the West, making those who would use the sacred plants to find their connection to the sacred criminals and outlaws. We are told that while we are free to *believe* that visionary medicines are sacred and a connection to the divine, we are not permitted to *practice*, as our practice is in conflict with other legal priorities, such as the so-called "war on drugs."

How would things be different if not just *belief* and *practice* were protected by law, but if *spiritual experience itself* were also protected? What I would like to argue is that *direct spiritual experience is the most intimate aspect of our religious or spiritual freedom and is central to our ability to freely explore our own spiritual natures.* In short, the primary argument here is that it is time to reframe the discussion. Direct spiritual experience should be a fundamental human right, and any law that would counter that right should be discarded as decidedly undemocratic and as curtailing our basic freedom as spiritual beings.

Belief is a decidedly poor foundation upon which to build a spiritual or religious tradition, especially in the modern world. Many of the beliefs upon which Western traditions are built don't hold up well against rationalism and scientific inquiry, especially when taken in their most dogmatic and fundamentalist forms. Much of the current debate in the West over science versus religion centers on this problem of belief and it promotes sloppy thinking on both sides. Religious leaders blindly dismiss scientific evidence when it conflicts with their cherished beliefs, wearing virtual blinders over their rational thinking, and scientists can be equally as naive, equating religion with mythological thinking and superstition and therefore needing to be dismissed as irrational and ultimately unreal. Both sides of this debate largely miss the fact that spiritual experience itself need not be based on any beliefs and that there are, in fact, many similarities between the claims of mystics, shamans, and scientists regarding the nature of reality when they are speaking from their direct experience rather than just repeating worn-out dogmas and long-cherished beliefs about reality and the way of the world.

Practice isn't necessarily any better as a foundation for a spiritual or religious tradition. One can practice – go to church, worship, pray, etc. – all one wants, but without a clear guide for how to achieve spiritual states of consciousness and cultivate a direct connection and experience of the sacred, one can simply "go through the motions" for one's entire life without ever having a genuine spiritual experience. Especially in our disenchanted world, religious liturgies and ritual forms can be empty and hollow, providing a social structure for religious practice, but very little in the way of actual spiritual experience. And even if one does manage to have a spiritual experience in such a tradition of practice, if in the West, it is very likely that one will also have someone in authority dictating what one is supposed to believe about the experience. And if one doesn't fit one's experience into pre-established dogmas, then one risks being branded a heretic or unbeliever in some form or another.

But what if we were truly free to choose how we wanted to explore our own spiritual natures, free from the constraints of dogmatic beliefs, strict ritual liturgies, and patronizing laws? What if we could, of our own free will, decide that we want to follow the path of entheogenic spirituality and use the sacred visionary medicines to enhance and explore our spiritual nature and cultivate our spiritual experiences as we saw fit? How would our society be different? How might things look if we had sovereignty over our minds?

Many contemporary religious practitioners claim that entheogenic spirituality is not true spirituality, not true religious practice. Sadly, such claims reflect a fairly profound ignorance of human history, culture, and religion. Altered states of consciousness, whether plant-induced or not, have been central to the development of spiritual and religious traditions from the very dawn of time. Dreams, trances, visions, and ecstatic states have formed the core of much of what has been passed down to us as religious traditions throughout history, and many of these altered states have been visionary plant-induced. This is an undeniable fact of history.

One can look virtually anywhere in the world at any point in history, and find the use of sacred plants and medicines to cultivate direct spiritual experience among shamans and mystics. It is fairly safe to say that humans have *always* made use of visionary plants, *wherever they are available*, to enhance their spiritual experience. In many respects, use of visionary plants and "religion" have been synonymous, especially where the emphasis is placed on direct spiritual experience rather than on the weaker foundations of belief and practice. However various religions may operate today, it is clear that their origins lie in the direct and immediate experiences of the shamans and mystics who inspired the religions in the first place. In short, the shamanic and mystical experience is both *prior to* and *originating of* religion itself. Without the altered states of consciousness and spiritual experiences of shamans and mystics, religion, as we know it, would simply not exist.

Religions in the West have largely feared shamans and shamanic practice. Mysticism in the West hasn't necessarily fared much better, but to some extent it was tolerated, though the Catholic Church branded some mystics as heretics and the mystery traditions were shunned and denigrated. Shamans were greeted with outright hostility, however, often being the targets of zealous Christian missionaries. Throughout Europe and the New World, countless shamans, witches, and healers were slaughtered at the hands of Christians, bent on stamping out any vestige of direct spiritual experience or practices that might be in conflict with the teachings of the Christian church. In Europe, that meant that thousands, if not millions, of women who practiced "witchcraft" were burned at the stake or otherwise killed. In the Americas, indigenous peoples were subjected to the brutality of genocide, ethnic cleansing, and the intentional murder of their shamanic leaders. According to Christian dogma, by definition, shamanic practitioners had to be devil worshipers, and therefore their murders were justified, along with those who followed them or refused to accept the Christian teachings, beliefs, and practices.

While shamans and shamanic traditions fared better in the East, they were not free from persecution from the spread of other religions. Many shamanic traditions were incorporated into Eastern religious traditions, such as the more trantric schools of Buddhism and Hinduism, but even here there was persecution of shamans. As trantric Buddhism spread through Asia, local shamans, who were often female, were treated as superstitious and ignorant. While they were not necessarily killed outright, as shamans and healers were at the hands of Christian missionaries, their practices were seen as less sophisticated and advanced than the complex trantric traditions that were largely male-dominated. It is only now that certain areas of Asia in the former Soviet Union are re-embracing shamanism, such as in the Republic of Tuva and Mongolia, both of which were heavily missionized by male Buddhist lamas.

It was not just Christians who were intolerant of shamans and other similar spiritual healing traditions in the West. With the advent of the Enlightenment and the Scientific Revolution, other dismissive and belittling attitudes towards shamans and spiritual experience in general became prominent in the West, the effects of which we are still living with today. In many ways, the Scientific Revolution was a reaction to the medieval scholasticism of Christian theologians, where all knowledge and proclamations of truth had to be subsumed under Christian dogma. Relying largely on Platonic and Aristotelian philosophy, Christian theologians made their models of reality conform to their pre-existing philosophical and theological postulations, rather than letting the evidence decide their models. For example, many religious leaders refused to look through Galileo's telescopes because the direct observation that the moon had varied features, as opposed to being a perfect, incorruptible sphere, as taught by Aristotelian philosophy and cosmology, would contradict their view of the world and universe. Scientists and rational thinkers, on the other hand, developed the relatively new view that observations about reality should inform our views on reality, not necessarily the other way around. If the moon is observed to be imperfect, then it is the theory that the moon is incorruptible that has to change, rather than the data should be denied and hidden away, as was the practice of the Church when observable facts contradicted their doctrine and theology.

One must also consider the esoteric origins of Western science, however, in order to understand its distinction from both the church and the folk traditions of Europe. Many early scientists were also magicians, astrologers, and alchemists, such as was the case with John Dee and Isaac Newton, among others. Alchemy was both an internal and external practice that sought correspondences between the manipulation of external metals and materials and the progression of spiritual awakening within the alchemist himself. It was alchemy that eventually gave rise to chemistry, just as astrology gave rise to astronomy, and natural philosophy gave birth to mechanics, physics, and biology. Thus, many of the roots of science were found within the Western esoteric traditions and secret societies, which were probably almost exclusively the province of privileged men within European societies.

Something quite significant is that, during the time of the Inquisition when the Catholic Church was busy exterminating local folk healers, the magicians, alchemists, and astrologers were largely left untouched and unharmed. A clear distinction was made between the "high" magicians and other esoteric practitioners who often taught at medieval universities and counseled heads of state and the aristocracy, and the "low" folk healers, midwives, "witches," and other local magical practitioners, most of whom were women. In short, the European patriarchy was clearly focused on removing the female non-Christian practitioners of direct spiritual practice but was far less concerned with the elite males who served the existing patriarchal power structure.

Thus the male elite survived the Inquisition and, through various transformations, became the leaders of the scientific revolution. However, with the growing success of "science" and the "scientific method" of careful observation, accumulation of data, and theory formation and revision, the more subjective aspects of magical practice were left aside and eventually relegated to the subjectivity of "religion," with the realm of objectivity left for science. With the philosopher Rene Descartes, we get a clear articulation of this view through his dualistic philosophy, clearly separating mind from body and the spiritual from the physical. Here, all things spiritual, subjective, and non-physical are given to religion, with observation of material facts through rational observation belonging to the province of science and scientific observation and theory building.

The result was that rationality and observation were seen as not only objective, and therefore verifiably true, but also as distinctly masculine traits. Under the scientific lens, nature was seen as feminine and the rational, male mind was viewed as the ultimate tool for unraveling the secrets of nature and providing domination over nature. In this sense, the scientific community reflected the same patriarchal misogyny of the Church in dominating women folk healers, making the feminine secondary and subject to the primacy of the masculine. And not only was nature feminine, but through masculine rationality, men were, in theory, able to dominate and control nature, bending "her" to their will.

We are still living with the effects of these forces of European society many hundreds of years later. The entire debate of the relationship or conflict between "religion" and "science" still bears the marks of this original divide. Science is seen to objectively deal with questions of the physical, while religion, at least according to scientists, should confine itself to the non-material and spiritual (which, according to many scientists, doesn't really exist anyway, so religion is therefore strictly mythical and imaginary, or simply a function of belief and practice with no factual connection to observable reality). So on one hand, we have objective, factual science that produces knowledge through supposedly purely objective means, and subjective, belief-based religion that does not promote subjective experience as much as it promotes adherence to beliefs and practices. When there is a conflict between the two views, as there often is, members of Western societies are basically forced to choose sides in this invented debate – either "objective truth" or "subjective belief" wins the day, with very little supposed meeting ground between the two. In short, we, in theory, have "knowledge" or "faith," one based on objectivity and the other blind belief.

Neither position has much room for subjective experience. According to the scientific view, subjective experiences cannot be objectively observed, and therefore are not open to questions of truth, theory building, model making, or any of the other standard procedures for producing "knowledge." Under this view, while a person may claim to have had a powerful spiritual experience, this is still theoretically subjective and therefore not amenable to the scientific worldview or system of practice. On the other hand, any subjective spiritual experience that does not fit within the confines of proscribed religious belief or doctrine is relegated to the bin of heresy, delusion, or devil worship.

These views were held fairly universally in the West until only relatively recently. In recent decades far more attention has been paid in the West to the practices, knowledge, and techniques of spiritual practitioners such as shamans, yogis, trantrikas, and others.

It is becoming increasingly clear that shamans, for example, hold a vast repository of knowledge relating to nearly all supposedly "scientific" subjects such as pharmacological properties of plants, ecological knowledge, astronomical knowledge, biology, medicine, and more. While there is still some dismissal of shamanic knowledge by mainstream rationalists and objectivists, overall, more respect for traditional knowledge is generally being shown within the larger society.

The same is also true of spiritual traditions that emphasize the cultivation of personal spiritual experience. Disillusioned by the hollow and empty teachings of the Western religions that emphasize largely irrational belief in the face of supposed scientific facts, many Westerners have turned to Eastern religions in the search for genuine spiritual experience and meaning. Taoism, Buddhism, Hinduism, yoga, tai chi, chi gong and many other Eastern practices have found willing and ready practitioners in the West, who find a very different emphasis in such traditions than what they have been traditionally offered in the West. Here, the emphasis is on each individual practitioner coming to their own spiritual realizations through their practice of meditation or spiritual exercise. While they may still be given various beliefs that are taught in conjunction with the given traditions, the overwhelming emphasis is on the direct experience itself.

Western societies still have a long way to go in their acceptance of subjective states of consciousness and personal spiritual practices. It is far more likely that a Western scientist will want to hook a Buddhist meditator up to a brain-scanning device than it is for the scientist to submit to a regimen of meditation and contemplation. The emphasis is still placed on the material side of the equation, with the Buddhist's neurobiology and neurochemistry being the focus of the scientific inquiry – not the value of the meditative experience and practice itself.

The same is largely true for Western science's appreciation for shamanic knowledge. Pharmaceutical companies are scrambling to learn the herbal wisdom of the shamans, but few are actually learning the methods of altered states of consciousness through which shamans have come to their hard-earned wisdom. While the West is genuinely recognizing that shamanic and traditional wisdom cannot be universally reduced to myth, legend and pre-scientific irrationality, the methods and techniques of shamans are still viewed as subjective and unscientific and therefore not necessarily worthy of emulation. The result is that while the physical and practical side of their knowledge is being widely accepted and appreciated at this time, their methods are still thought to be too subjective to be considered scientific.

We can see a shift toward the value of direct spiritual experience, however. Because this has been sorely lacking in contemporary Western traditions, Westerners have sought their sources of direct spiritual experience elsewhere. However, even among those who seek to follow a mystical or shamanic path, there is still some fear and denigration of visionary medicines as genuine spiritual tools. Oddly, many contemporary Western shamanic practitioners claim that genuine shamanism does not use visionary plants, despite the historical and cultural fact that visionary medicines are used or have been used by countless shamanic cultures across the world. Many mainstream "shamanic practitioners" claim that their practice is "drug free" and instead make use of "shamanic drumming" and other widely practiced New Age-style techniques such as visualization, guided imagery, and the like. Similarly, those involved in meditation traditions often proclaim that visionary plants are "short-cuts" or "false awakenings," and that only through years of dedicated meditation and study can one have a genuine spiritual experience or mystical awakening. So, in both cultural streams, there is still resistance to visionary plants and medicines, despite their place in both history and contemporary shamanic cultures.

The result is that, even among so-called "alternative" spiritual practitioners, there is still a fairly strong bias against visionary plants and medicines, sometimes even more so than among mainstream culture, as efforts are made by these alternative traditions to distinguish themselves from the more "questionable" practices of entheogenic spirituality. Thus despite the cultural shift, entheogens are still underground as spiritual tools in the West, and remain largely illegal to use, and even when legal, are still considered with great suspicion along with the judgment that such a path is somehow illegitimate or not genuine. Entheogenic spirituality is viewed as somehow being make-believe, imaginary, and hedonistic. It is not considered to be a real spiritual path.

When it comes to the spiritual use of visionary plants, spiritual seekers find that not only do they have to fight against the mainstream of Western history and culture, but also have to fight against restrictive and often discriminatory laws concerning the use of visionary plants and medicines. Ever since Timothy Leary and his colleagues at Harvard unleashed LSD on the West, we have been living with the repercussion of an irrational, dogmatic, and I would argue, unconstitutional "war on drugs," which has caught many of the sacred visionary medicines in its net. Those who would seek to expand their horizons by seeking genuine direct spiritual experience through entheogens have to risk not only social scorn and punishment, but also the threat of jail and losing everything in their lives including their homes, property, families, jobs, and place within society. The war on drugs has put more people in jail than any other social program and is largely responsible for the fact that U.S. has the largest prison population on the planet, with a greater percentage of our citizens locked up behind bars than any other country in the world. It has also been used to promote repressive and intrusive police tactics and is often used as a means of imprisoning minority populations, with people of color being far more likely to be imprisoned for drug use or possession than caucasians. While it is likely the case that most people jailed for drug use are not necessarily seeking to use these substances for spiritual purposes, it is undoubtedly true that some are, and for some it literally is a matter of religious freedom in that they are being punished for consuming what in their tradition is considered a ceremonial sacrament.

How can this be the case? Even if we want to punish people for taking drugs, why is it that the ceremonial and sacramental use of visionary plants and medicines is largely illegal? Why isn't an individual's choice of sacrament a protected activity under our laws? Why do we not seem to have a legally protected right to pursue and cultivate direct spiritual experience however we see fit, as long as our actions do not cause any immediate or direct harm to others?

From the brief overview of historical forces outlined above, it is not difficult to see that anyone in the West wanting to use a visionary sacrament would have a great deal of historical, social, and cultural inertia to overcome in order for their choice to be accepted by mainstream institutions. But it is not just acceptance that we are considering here, but the actual legal recognition of a right to practice legitimate spiritual pursuits as one sees fit. Only naturally, the laws of our country have come out of the same historical stream as our scientific and religious institutions, and therefore the views of science and religion have had a direct impact on how we conceive of constitutionally protected activities and how we define what categories of choices deserve the protection of law.

When one considers the legal issues surrounding the sacramental use of entheogens, it is easy to see that the significance of *cultivating direct spiritual experience* is nowhere taken into consideration. Rather, we are confronted with issues of "belief" and "practice," and rather narrow definitions of what characterizes freedom in the pursuit of a religious or spiritual practice. To understand how this functions in contemporary American society, we can now turn to examine some of our legal institutions and practices and how they impinge upon one's right to explore spirituality as one sees fit.

Let us start with the United States constitution and the supposed freedoms that it guarantees for all U.S. citizens. As the First Amendment reads: "Congress shall make no law respecting an establishment of religion, or prohibiting the free exercise thereof." The first part of this amendment addresses the fact that European immigrants to the U.S. were often coming from countries that had official state religions, such as the Anglican Church of England. This amendment was created to insure that there would be no official religion of the U.S., despite the claims of many evangelicals that the U.S. is a "Christian" country. In short, it reads that the federal government cannot require any U.S. citizen to belong to any particular religion, or any religion at all. We are all free to believe and practice as we see fit and cannot be compelled into any particular religion, as was the case in Europe. The second part limits the government's ability to interfere with whatever religious tradition we freely chose to become a part of, clearly stating that the government cannot interfere with one's ability to practice their chosen religion. This amendment immediately reflects back to the experience of European immigrants to the New World, many of whom came specifically seeking religious freedom due to the persecution they faced in their home countries in Europe. The U.S. was to be the land of religious liberty where people could believe and practice however they saw fit according to their own conscience and desire.

The first immediate problem with this amendment is that it inspires us to question what defines a "religion." Religions are generally understood to be institutions that have accepted beliefs, practices, rituals, hierarchies, sacred texts, ceremonial calendars, etc., but virtually no emphasis is placed on direct spiritual experience when defining religious practice or experience. We therefore have a somewhat restrictive view of what constitutes a "religion" per se or what should be taken into consideration when defining or recognizing a religion. It also raises the question of who gets to decide what is accepted as a "religion" or not, with the answer being that it is the government itself that gets to decide who meets their criteria for a "religion," despite the fact that the government shall make no law respecting the establishment of religion. While it is true that the government has certainly refrained from compelling our allegiance to any particular religion, it is also true that it is the government that gets to decide which practices and institutions merit the designation of religion in the first place, which could be construed as "respecting an establishment of religion."

Thus the first amendment is not without its problems and is not as clear-cut a protection as it may seem. It is all the more problematic when one is looking at questions of "spiritual" practice as opposed to "religious" practice. This is especially true when one considers shamanism and mysticism. Neither shamans nor mystics need to be a part of any particular religion at all for them to pursue their spiritual aims, and has often historically been the case in the West, the shamans and mystics have been purposely excluded from our institutions of religion and religious practice. They can therefore constitute a class of spiritual practitioners who are not participating in any given "religion," at least not as defined within U.S. law.

If shamans and mystics and their practices already fall somewhat outside the definitions of protected activities under U.S. law, we can only imagine how much more challenging it would be for a solitary practitioner of entheogenic spirituality to make a case that his or her practices should be protected by the constitution. Not only would such a person have to argue for why their practices are "religious" in the first place, but would also have to argue for why laws created to prohibit the use of illegal "drugs" should be disregarded in their case in order to protect their "religious freedom." To this date, no one has ever successfully argued in U.S. court that their personal choice to use an entheogenic sacrament to cultivate their personal spiritual experience is protected by the constitution. And unless we carefully examine what we are protecting and how, it is unlikely that anyone ever will succeed in making such an argument before the U.S. Supreme Court.

It is my contention that *direct spiritual experience* should be a protected category of activity as defined and delineated in the U.S. constitution or other similar political documents. And even beyond the U.S., I would propose that it be written into a fundamental declaration of human rights for the United Nations and be applicable to all nations of the world. Given that our direct and immediate spiritual experience is the most intimate aspect of our beings, perhaps even more intimate that our physical bodies, our right to direct spiritual experience should be protected, and not just our right to participate in a religion of our choice. There is a difference between being spiritually aware and active and being religious, but we have absolutely no protections for spiritual experience, even though our constitution protects religious freedom. And even when we protect religious freedom, there are other considerations that are thrown into the mix so that one can never assume that just because a practice or belief is part of a religion that it will be protected, as will be shown in the analysis of U.S. Supreme Court case given below.

Before we look at the Supreme Court, however, I would like to add that if direct spiritual experience were a protected class of activity, then so would the spiritual use of entheogenic sacraments. Any argument that use of entheogens cannot be spiritual is clearly contradicted by the overwhelming evidence of world history and human cultures. Only someone truly ignorant or intentionally misleading of the role of entheogens across human history and cultures would venture the statement that entheogens cannot be spiritual. Personally, I consider the argument to be moot. If you know the facts, then you know that entheogens have been part of the human spiritual experience since the very dawn of human culture and continue to be to this day. It is not an opinion or a belief. It is simply the way things are and to argue otherwise is incorrect and uninformed. There is no debate here. The facts are in and they are clear.

But to see how the Supreme Court deals with constitutional issues surrounding entheogen use, consider the "Smith" case that was decided in 1990. In this case an employee for the state of Oregon lost his job and his benefits when he admitted to using peyote in a Native American Church ceremony. Smith made the case that he was merely exercising his constitutionally protected right to the free exercise of religion, as guaranteed by the first amendment. While peyote may be a schedule I illegal drug in the eyes of U.S. law, as a member of a legally recognized church that makes use of the peyote cactus as a sacrament, he felt that he was unjustly punished by the state of Oregon. The state of Oregon, on the other hand, made the case that peyote is illegal in Oregon under federal law and the state was merely fulfilling its duty to apply the law equally to all citizens. Smith's argument for religious freedom was trumped by the state's interest in upholding federal and local drug laws.

Smith lost his case in Oregon, and eventually the Supreme Court took up the case. The result was that Smith lost and the court found on behalf of the state of Oregon. Justice Antoine Scalia wrote the majority opinion for the court, stating the following:

> The free exercise of religion means, first and foremost, the right to *believe* and profess whatever religious doctrine one desires. . .

> [The respondents] assert that "prohibiting the free exercise [of religion]" includes requiring any individual to observe a generally applicable law that requires (or forbids) the performance of an act that his religious belief forbids (or requires).

> It is a permissible reading of the text . . . to say that if prohibiting the exercise of religion . . . is not the object of the [law] but merely the incidental effect of a generally applicable and otherwise valid provision, the First Amendment has not been offended.

> To make an individual's obligation to obey such a law contingent upon the law's coincidence with his *religious beliefs*, except where the State's interest is "compelling" - permitting him, by virtue of his *beliefs*, to become a law unto himself, contradicts both constitutional tradition and common sense.

> If the "compelling interest" test is to be applied at all, then, it must be applied across the board, to all actions thought to be religiously commanded. Moreover, if "compelling interest" really means what it says (and watering it down here would subvert its rigor in the

other fields where it is applied), many laws will not meet the test.
Any society adopting such a system would be courting *anarchy* . . .
The First Amendment's protection of religious liberty does not
require this.
(Employment Division of Oregon v. Smith, emphasis added)

It is quite telling that, in his argument, Justice Scalia
emphasized the two pillars of *practice* and *belief*, as definitions of
religious freedom. He does not address *why* Smith is using peyote.
He uses it not because he "believes" in peyote: he believes in peyote
because *it produces direct spiritual experience*. Rather, Scalia is
addressing how the imposition of drug laws affect Smith's ability to
practice as he believes he should. And in rendering his decision,
Scalia clearly states that expecting the government to grant exceptions
to the law according to an individual's religious belief would "be
courting anarchy." Though Scalia does not say as much, what he
seems to be indicating is that *true* freedom would render people
ungovernable. If we could all make up our minds for ourselves
according to our own understanding of religious practice, it would be
impossible to expect people to obey the law and anarchy would reign.
Scalia seems to be of the opinion that this would be a bad thing. He is
also of the opinion that the constitution clearly does *not* protect
religious practice and belief uniformly and universally, but only in
consideration with other existing laws when those laws were not
written with specific discriminatory intent (such as a law intentionally
written to target a specific religion, group, or ethnicity). Because the
law against peyote was not written to discriminate against Native
American use of peyote and applies to all races equally, Smith,
according to Scalia, could not claim that peyote laws were unfairly
burdening his culturally based religion.

Scalia's decision gave rise to some profound questions, the
most significant of which was: if a person can lose his rights for
participating in a legally recognized religion that uses a psychedelic
sacrament, then what real protection is there for any religion? Is there
any substance at all to the First Amendment, or can the government
simply trump religious freedom whenever a religion's practices come
into conflict with existing U.S. law? Here, the burden was placed on
Smith to show that the government should uphold his First
Amendment rights and not the other way around. The government
did not have to show why drug laws were more inviolable than the

Constitution. Given that this is was the case, what teeth does the Constitution then have to limit the actions of the government? According to Scalia, apparently none at all, for it would lead to "anarchy."

The result of Scalia's decision in Employment Division vs. Smith was the creation and enactment of the Religious Freedom Restoration Act of 1993 as created by Congress and signed into law by President Bill Clinton. The Religious Freedom Restoration Act (RFRA) was a direct response to this frightening Supreme Court decision that seemed to strip the Constitution of any real ability to protect the rights of citizens in the face of government interference with their granted liberties. The main thrust of the RFRA is that the burden of proof and argument must be placed on the government in religious liberty cases, rather than the reversal that Scalia argued for in placing the burden on the one whose rights were violated. Specifically, the RFRA reads:

The Congress finds that--

(1) the framers of the Constitution, recognizing free exercise of religion as an unalienable right, secured its protection in the First Amendment to the Constitution;

(2) laws 'neutral' toward religion may burden religious exercise as surely as laws intended to interfere with religious exercise;

(3) governments should not substantially burden religious exercise without compelling justification;

(4) in Employment Division v. Smith, 494 U.S. 872 (1990) the Supreme Court virtually eliminated the requirement that the government justify burdens on religious exercise imposed by laws neutral toward religion; and

(5) the compelling interest test as set forth in prior Federal court rulings is a workable test for striking sensible balances between religious liberty and competing prior governmental interests.

(b) Purposes: The purposes of this Act are--

(1) to restore the compelling interest test as set forth in Sherbert v. Verner, 374 U.S. 398 (1963) and Wisconsin v. Yoder, 406 U.S. 205 (1972) and to guarantee its application in all cases where free exercise of religion is substantially burdened; and

(2) to provide a claim or defense to persons whose religious exercise is substantially burdened by government.

SEC. 3. FREE EXERCISE OF RELIGION PROTECTED.

(a) In General: Government shall not substantially burden a person's exercise of religion even if the burden results from a rule of general applicability, except as provided in subsection (b).

(b) Exception: Government may substantially burden a person's exercise of religion only if it demonstrates that application of the burden to the person--

(1) is in furtherance of a compelling governmental interest; and

(2) is the least restrictive means of furthering that compelling governmental interest.

(c) Judicial Relief: A person whose religious exercise has been burdened in violation of this section may assert that violation as a claim or defense in a judicial proceeding and obtain appropriate relief against a government. Standing to assert a claim or defense under this section shall be governed by the general rules of standing under article III of the Constitution

Despite the fact that the RFRA was inspired by a court case that dealt with a person's legal right to consume an illegal visionary plant, in this case peyote, the RFRA does not address the issue of entheogens in any direct way. Because it does not directly address entheogens, or the purpose for which they are used, namely *to produce direct spiritual experiences*, the general role of entheogens as sacraments as a protected category of activity still has not been addressed by Congress. Instead, we are given guidelines for how the government is to consider cases of infringement of religious liberty without any clear procedures or considerations specifically for entheogenic sacraments. Therefore, while the RFRA helped to define and protect Native Americans' rights to use peyote in the Native

American Church, the protection for use of entheogenic sacraments was not extended beyond the special case of Native Americans and their legal rights. In other words, the protections were not made universal and in fact were quite limited and specific in their scope. Since that time, both the Uniao Do Vegetal and the Santo Daime churches, both of which use ayahuasca as a sacrament, have argued their cases in court, but these too are limited in application as the cases did not involve questions of individual rights outside of a recognized religion.

One limitation with the RFRA is that we are still dealing with the concept of "religion" and do not, as of yet, have any legal guidelines for addressing questions of individual spiritual practice. The basic assumption made under U.S. law is that "religion" is a protected category whereas individual spiritual practice that is not directly tied to a "religion" is not even taken into consideration as a possible protected category. Therefore the RFRA does not seem to have much applicability for those interested in arguing that their personal and non-religious, though spiritual, use of entheogens should be a protected class of activity.

What if Smith had not been a member of the Native American Church and simply an individual who chose to consume peyote as a sacrament for personal spiritual growth and experience? Would the RFRA have helped him? Most likely not, for then Smith would not have been able to argue that his practices were part of a "religion" per se, unless he wanted to make the argument that mysticism or shamanism, or even direct spiritual experience itself, were "religions." None of these meet the general criteria for religion as defined in U.S. law, however, so it is unlikely that the court would have accepted his argument, for do so would be to open up the question of "anarchy" that Scalia wrote of in his opinion. With a "religion," the court can look to what the professed beliefs and practices of the institution are and judge whether an individual is actually practicing that religion in accordance with its doctrines and traditions. When it comes to individual practice, the court has nothing to evaluate a person's claim with and must either take the person's word as genuine or dismiss it as an excuse. For example, virtually anyone could claim that his or her illegal use of entheogens was "spiritual," but by what means would the court assess the validity of such a claim? How could they know that a person was genuine?

By what means could they evaluate such a claim of legal protection? And furthermore, why would they bother, given that individual spiritual practice is not yet a protected category?

Of course all this would be obviated were the prohibition against entheogens to end, and this would be the easiest solution. We could simply recognize that competent adults are free to make up their own minds about what they choose to put into their bodies and for what reason and leave it at that. Entheogen use could be made legal, regulated to prevent minors from gaining access to entheogens, and used by freely consenting adults as long as that use did not cause any direct harm to others.

However, given that entheogen use is unlikely to be made legal at a general level any time soon, it would seem that attempting to reframe the argument about protected categories of practice, namely the proposal that we consider individual spiritual practice and direct spiritual experience as protected categories, might be a more fruitful avenue of addressing the issue. For entheogens could still be illegal as a general law, but their use for spiritual purposes could be made a protected category just as peyote consumption is still illegal, yet it is a protected activity for members of the Native American Church. With some amendments to the RFRA, or the introduction of a similar act that specifically addresses the centrality of individual spiritual experience, this could be a realistic goal. My proposal is that we need a clear statement of rights along the lines of what I outline below (keeping in mind that I am neither a Constitutional scholar nor a lawyer or legislator).

THE UNIVERSAL DECLARATION OF THE HUMAN RIGHT TO DIRECT SPIRITUAL EXPERIENCE

We recognize the following:

Human beings are innately spiritual. The human quest for spiritual meaning and experience is fundamental to the human experience. Personal spiritual experience is furthermore understood to be one of the most intimate aspects of person's identity, sense of self, and worldview.

While the human quest for spiritual meaning and experience can be institutionalized through the formation and continuation of religious traditions, the drive for spiritual meaning and experience is not limited to religious activity or membership *per se*.

Religious practice and membership is not identical to spiritual experience. Religion, as a social institution, provides opportunity for like-minded people to gather together in groups to collectively express their beliefs in the context of shared practices. Religion provides structures of ritual, ceremony, religious teachings, and a community of similarly-oriented individuals. Within the context of a religion, persons may be afforded the opportunity for direct spiritual experience, but this is not necessarily the case. As direct spiritual experience is primarily an individual matter, the locus of spiritual experience is necessarily the individual, and not a religious tradition or institution.

While religious membership and activity is universally recognized as a fundamental human right and is protected by law, individual pursuit of spiritual experiences has not been afforded the same legal protections. This act seeks to correct this omission from the list of universal human rights.

Because the locus of direct spiritual experience is the individual, protections for individual spiritual experience must be afforded directly to individuals, rather than to the institutions in which they practice. As a result, protection for direct spiritual experience is not limited to individuals who are members of religious traditions, but extend equally to all individuals, regardless of religious affiliation or lack thereof.

All practices that contribute to an individual's cultivation of direct spiritual experience are hereby affirmed to be protected by international laws recognizing universal human rights, with the condition that such practices do not violate any other universally recognized human rights of other persons, such as the rights to life, liberty, and pursuit of happiness.

In recognition of this universal human right to direct spiritual experience, it is hereby decreed that no government shall persecute or punish any individual who chooses to pursue the cultivation of direct spiritual experience in a manner that is respectful of the human rights of others.

It is furthermore recognized that the universal human right to direct spiritual experience provides a legal defense for those who would choose to pursue the use of entheogenic agents in their quest to achieve direct spiritual experience. While recognizing that governments have a vested interest in reducing the impact of recreational drug use and abuse within their territories, drug laws, in and of themselves, are not sufficient grounds for baring the legitimate use of entheogenic sacraments for personal spiritual experience.

The burden of proof for the limiting of any activity that can be construed as the cultivation of direct personal spiritual experience is clearly placed on any regulating body, governmental or otherwise. The universal right to direct spiritual experience will be afforded to all equally without any interference by regulating bodies unless said regulating bodies can demonstrate beyond any doubt that the activities of any individual is in violation of the fundamental human rights of another person or persons. Claiming that an individual's practice, such as might be the case with the use of entheogens, is against any law, is not sufficient grounds for disallowing the practice. The standard for the burden of proof is to be judged solely on how any given practice violates the rights of others.

It is my hope that the issues raised and arguments provided in this essay demonstrate why such a declaration of human rights is not only necessary, but also valid and reasonable as well. If we truly want to be free, then it is only reasonable that we be afforded our freedoms to pursue our spiritual connection to the divine however we may see fit, as long as our practices do not interfere with the rights of others. Obviously, such a claim could be made for the use of entheogens in general, and not just confined to a spiritual context, for just as our pursuit of spiritual consciousness and experience should be a fundamental human right, so should our experience of *any* level of consciousness that does not impinge on the rights of others be so protected. However, as I am primarily concerned with spiritual consciousness in this essay, I have chosen to focus on this more specific case of rights here. I am certainly of the view that people should be free to affect their consciousness as they see fit, regardless of whether it is done for spiritual purposes or not. However, given that religion is already a protected category, extending similar protections to direct spiritual experience might be an easier path to take, given current drug laws. Cognitive liberty in general is a fight worth fighting, and I fully support it. Yet, it is my contention that recognition of the legal right to spiritual experience might have the effect of obviating drug laws in their application to individuals who seek to use entheogens for spiritual experience.

SANTO DAIME AND RELIGIOUS FREEDOM, MARCH 2009

In September of 2008, a small group of defenders of genuine religious freedom decided that it was time to bring their case before a federal judge and have the U.S. government officially recognize their right to practice their religion without threat of punishment or imprisonment. The leadership of Church of the Holy Light of the Queen (CHLQ) in Ashland, Oregon, as lead by *padrinho* Jonathan Goldman, made the daring choice to take the government to court to protect their religious freedom. Not surprisingly, the case was decided in CHLQ's favor in March of 2009.

CHLQ is a North American branch of the Santo Daime religion, which originates from Brazil. The primary focus of the Santo Daime religion is the sacramental ingestion of the *daime* drink, which is the religion's name for ayahuasca. While recognized as a legal religion in Brazil, Santo Daime has not been recognized as having a legal right to the ingestion of daime in the United States by the federal government due to the fact that it contains a controlled substance, DMT.

The Religious Freedom Restoration Act (RFRA) makes it quite clear that simply claiming that a substance violates federal drug laws does not grant the government the right to prohibit the free exercise of religion outright and that any such prohibition requires a strict burden of proof on the part of the government. In bringing forth their case, CHLQ argued that the RFRA clearly protects their right to drink daime and practice their religion without threat of incarceration from the government. The result of the case is that the court agreed with CHLQ.

This case is significant not only because it affirmed the religious freedom of members of the Santo Daime religion, but also because it highlights how little substance there is to government sponsored prohibitions of ceremonial use of entheogens. On virtually every argument presented by the defendants, the judge ruled that the government provided "no evidence" and relied on "speculation." In short, the judge was not convinced by a single argument put forth by the government in their attempt to curtail religious freedom. A sample of quotes from the "Finding of facts" makes this clear:

Defendants have not presented evidence that Daime tea is addictive or causes long-term health problems. (page 9)

Defendants' experts raise the possibility that Daime tea could cause acute or long-term psychosis. However, defendants rely more on speculation than empirical evidence to support this assertion. (page 11)

Defendants argue that consuming Daime tea could be fatal. However, defendants have not presented evidence that Daime tea or hoasca has caused any deaths (page 15)

Defendants submit evidence regarding two deaths, neither of which had anything to do with Daime tea or hoasca. (page 16)

Defendants raise other possible dangers, based largely on extrapolation from studies of other drugs and on speculation. (page 16)

Defendants have not presented evidence that plaintiffs have ever allowed Daime tea to be used without the church's authorization. (page 17)

The government cites the potential danger to children. There is no evidence that children were harmed when given token amounts of Daime tea. (page 20)

The government also asserts a compelling interest in preventing diversion to recreational use. The government has not presented evidence that there is a significant market for Daime tea. (page 20)

The government has failed to show that outright prohibition of the Daime tea is the least restrictive mean of furthering its interests. (page 21)

As can be seen from the above quotes, Judge Owen Panner, who presided over this case and is the author of the above quotes, determined that the government did not introduce a single piece of compelling evidence. On each count, he rejected the government's argument as based on speculation and as entirely lacking in evidence. This was a clear case of religious freedom and as a result, the Santo Daime church has had its right to daime affirmed in U.S. federal court.

What would happen if a practitioner of Amazonian shamanism, which has made use of ayahuasca (the same drink as the daime) for far longer than the Santo Daime religion went to court with the aim of using the RFRA? Is ayahuasca shamanism a religion? Do shamans and individual practitioners have rights equal to those who practice within official "churches"? Ayahuasca has been used religiously and spiritually for thousands of years, as opposed to the 70 – 80 year history of the Santo Daime church. Does not reason and equal protection under the law necessitate that individual practitioners be recognized as having the same fundamental rights?

The decision in the Santo Daime case is a good one, but much more work needs to be done at the legal level. It is terribly ironic that a relatively new religion has earned its legal right to a medicine that has been used for thousands of years by indigenous people who would not be afforded the same right were they to attempt to practice their religions and traditions openly in the U.S. The time to keep pushing the envelope is now.

Who will be bold enough to stand up for genuine freedom? Who else is daring enough to follow the paths blazed by the Native American Church, the UDV and Santo Daime? Who will affirm that the *oldest* spiritual traditions of shamanism and sacred plant use are also worthy of equal protection under the law – perhaps even more so, given their antiquity?

The tide is turning. Truth, justice, equality and freedom are on our side. Are you ready to ride the wave?

ENDNOTE:

Personally, I would like to thank Jonathan and Jane Goldman and the entire congregation of the Church of the Holy Light of the Queen. I first had the pleasure to attend a Work in April of 2008. Since then, I have been honored to attend many Works and drink daime, something that has had a profound impact on my life. What I experienced at the church was a community of sincere and devoted individuals worshiping and experiencing the divine together in a healthy and respectful way. That these good people have affirmed their inalienable right to practice their religion without fear of imprisonment or governmental harassment is a tremendous triumph. I applaud their bravery and determination to move their case forward and give thanks to the daime for all that it has given me.

ALSO BY MARTIN W. BALL, PH.D.

available at www.martinball.net

*The Entheogenic Evolution: Psychedelics,
Consciousness and Awakening
the Human Spirit*

Kyandara Publishing, 2008

ISBN: 978-0-578-00228-6

*Sage Spirit: Salvia Divinorum and the
Entheogenic Experience*

Kyandara Publishing, 2007

ISBN: 978-0-615-15708-5

*Mushroom Wisdom: How Shamans Cultivate
Spiritual Consciousness*

Ronin Publishing, 2006

ISBN: 978-1-579-51036-7

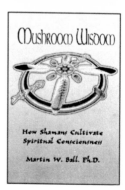

Martin W. Ball has a Ph.D. in Religious Studies with an emphasis on Native American traditions and shamanism. *Entheologues* is his fourth book on entheogenic spirituality. Dr. Ball currently lives in Ashland, Oregon and is busy developing an entheogenic paradigm for the nature of reality. His books, music and original artwork can be found at www.martinball.net.

THE ENTHEOGENIC EVOLUTION PODCAST

with host, Dr. Martin Ball, is available at iTunes and www.entheogenic.podomatic.com

This weekly podcast features interviews with leading entheogenic thinkers and researchers, information on the spiritual use of entheogens, and discussions of indigenous shamanic practices.

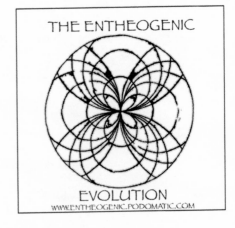

Breinigsville, PA USA
07 February 2010
232089BV00001B/135/P